This book is dedicated by the authors and by the Campaign for an Independent Britain to the memory of the Rt Hon. Lord Jay of Battersea (1907–1996), late president of the Campaign.

He brought intellectual rigour to the European debate, was a tireless campaigner and a generous source of advice.

BLOOMFIELD BOOKS
26 Meadow Lane
SUDBURY
Suffolk
ENGLAND CO10 6TD
Tel: Sudbury (01787) 376374

Biography

Brian Burkitt is a Senior Lecturer in Economics at the University of Bradford. In November 1974 and April 1975 he wrote two widely-quoted reports, *Britain and the European Economic Community: An Economic Re-Appraisal,* and *Britain and the European Economic Community: A Political Re-Appraisal,* published by British Business for World Markets. He is also author of *Trade Unions and Wages* (1975), *Trade Unions and the Economy* (1979), *Radical Political Economy* (1984), and over one hundred articles in learned journals. He has previously co-authored *What 1992 Really Means: Single Market or Double Cross?* (1989) and *From Rome to Maastricht* (1992) for the Campaign for an Independent Britain. He is a frequent contributor and commentator on economic issues to television and radio programmes.

Mark Baimbridge is a Lecturer in Economics at the University of Bradford. He co-authored *What 1992 Really Means: Single Market or Double Cross?* (1989) and *From Rome to Maastricht* (1992) for the Campaign for an Independent Britain. He has published over fifty articles, mainly concerning Britain's relationship with the EU, in learned and current affairs journals in economics, sociology, politics and social policy. He has recently submitted his PhD thesis on Britain's membership of the EU. He is a frequent contributor and commentator on economic issues to radio and in newspapers.

Philip Whyman is a Research Assistant at the University of Bradford. He recently completed research leading to the degree of PhD and subsequently co-authored *There **is** an Alternative.* His research interests include the economic development of the Scandinavian countries, with particular emphasis on Sweden, and the UK's future role in the EU. He has published over a dozen articles in learned journals and a number of policy papers.

There *is* an alternative

Britain and its relationship with the EU

Brian Burkitt

Mark Baimbridge

Philip Whyman

CAMPAIGN FOR AN INDEPENDENT BRITAIN

British Library Cataloguing-in-Publication Data.
A catalogue for this book is available from the British Library.

There is an alternative
Britain and its relationship with the EU
ISBN 0 9519642 1 6
First published April 1996

© Copyright 1996 Burkitt, Baimbridge & Whyman

Published by: The Campaign for an Independent Britain,
81 Ashmole Street, London SW8 1NF

Origination by: Nelson & Pollard, Oxford
Printed by: Joshua Horgan, Oxford

Contents

Preface

by the Rt Hon. Norman Lamont, MP

I am delighted to commend this clear and challenging contribution to the European debate. The authors are to be congratulated for puncturing so many myths and slaughtering quite a few sacred cows.

There are some good points in this book with which I disagree. I do not share all the analysis of the consequences of EU membership. I certainly do not agree with their views on so-called 'deindustrialisation'.

But it would be difficult for anyone to disagree with their view of the Common Agricultural Policy or the disaster that goes under the name of the Common Fisheries Policy. The authors quite rightly point to the irony than from the moment Britain decided to tie itself to Europe, the European economy became one of the slowest growing in the world. And yet for Britain, much more than for our European partners, the rest of the world in Asia and North America matters.

Dr Johnson once remarked that "Most opinions are held because they are in fashion." The problem about European debate is that for a long time it has been difficult to get a fair hearing for detached or dispassionate views. It is extraordinary that a Government Minister should say that it is not necessary because the benefits are self-evident. They are not. There are advantages and disadvantages and in any intelligent debate they should both be examined.

The authors rightly examine different models for Britain's relationship with Europe, including the Swiss and Norwegian. There must be ways of getting the advantages of free trade without getting dragged down into further political integration of the kind sought by our partners in Europe but overwhelmingly rejected by the British people.

The British public have been scared into believing that there are no alternatives. All the time we are told there cannot be any monetary sovereignty for a country like Britain. We are doomed to be dominated by German interest rates. But why is it that Switzerland has been able to have both lower interest rates and lower inflation than Germany?

The nation state remains the best, most well-tried way of governing people. Nowhere except in Europe is the nation state questioned. As the authors say, the impact of globalisation on nation states is highly exaggerated. The nation state is perfectly capable of dealing with most problems. The few problems that are beyond its capacity will not be within the control of regional blocs either.

The European debate is approaching its climax in this country. What is at stake is the right of the people in democracies to govern themselves. That is why this book is a highly useful contribution to an overwhelmingly important issue.

Rt Hon. Norman Lamont, MP

Foreword

by the Rt Hon. Peter Shore, MP

In the post war period, Britain's policy makers have had their successes and their failures; but there have been two mistakes of genuinely historic and strategic importance.

The first was the failure to attend the Messina Conference in 1955 and thus to miss the opportunity, from the position of strength that we then held as the leading European power, of putting our own stamp and shape on the foundations of what was soon to become the Treaty of Rome. The federal institutions and the Euro-protectionist policies for agriculture and industrial trade which were then created could and should have been vetoed and never seen the light of day.

The second and still more damaging strategic policy failure was Heath's decision to join – from a position of relative weakness – the European Economic community in 1973.

In this pamphlet, *"There Is An Alternative"*, Messrs Burkitt, Baimbridge and Whyman show just how much membership has cost us over the past 22 years. Our trade with the European countries, previously in surplus, has now turned into a cumulative nightmare deficit of no less than £87 billion – equivalent to £145 billion at today's prices. In addition, for the privilege of membership we have paid taxes to the EEC for each year of our membership far in excess of any receipts from the European budget; indeed our contributions total a massive £30 billion net. In spite of Mrs Thatcher's famous rebates, in 1994/5 we paid just under £2.5 billion to the European Union and the forecast contributions for 1995/6 is just under £3.5 billion. That is not all. The authors describe and measure another component: the cost to Britain of our two year membership of the Exchange Rate Mechanism – which we joined under pressure from the European

Community in October 1990 and which market pressures forced us to leave in September 1992. But not before we had lost a million more jobs, nearly 4% of our GDP and suffered vast losses to our gold and dollar reserves in a vain attempt to defend sterling within its ERM parity. The cost of this venture the authors price at not less than £68 billion.

The great threat which now confronts us and which the authors analyse and expose is the implementation of the Maastricht Treaty. If we do join a single currency it would be an act of folly, economic and political, without parallel in our history. For, if we give up our own currency, if we turn the Bank of England into an agent and subsidiary of the European Central Bank in Frankfurt, if we put government borrowing, taxation and expenditure under the rule of a Treaty, we lose all effective control over our own economy, destroy meaningful democratic self-government in Britain and take a giant step towards a federal Europe.

Finally, as the title of this pamphlet makes clear, the authors have the courage to think the unthinkable; they examine a range of alternative relationships between Britain and the European Union: from "this far and no further" through the Norwegian and Swiss models to total withdrawal.

These alternatives deserve the closest study, in the knowledge that a major change in our national strategy requires great determination and far-sighted thinking by both political leaders and the people. But, as the authors rightly say, "the prize is great": no less than our prosperity, our democracy and the continued independence of the United Kingdom.

Rt Hon. Peter Shore, MP

Introduction

The European Union (EU) was designed to achieve the noble goal of preventing another European war whilst creating a European superpower of equal size and importance to the USA, thereby giving all its people real influence over world affairs. The UK's entry was to create an economic nirvana of faster economic growth and improved export opportunities within a trade area characterised by standardised regulations and the free movement of goods, services, labour and capital. The Single Internal Market (SIM) was intended to remove remaining non-tariff barriers, thus providing greater potential economies of scale. These would further stimulate economic growth, whilst economic and monetary union (EMU) would bring the additional benefits of lower transaction costs and greater business certainty. Yet, if the 'European Project' has been so positive for the UK economy and for all the European people, why is there a growing sense of unease and opposition to further integration across Europe?

The answer is that, almost without exception, the promises made to secure a 'Yes' vote in the 1975 referendum and continued acquiescence to membership thereafter were, on a charitable interpretation grossly exaggerated, and less generously, calculated deceit. In 1971 Edward Heath told us that the EU was not a "federation of provinces or countries" and there was "no question of any erosion of essential national sovereignty" (Cmnd. 4715). However, two decades later, the primacy of European law over those passed by our own democratically elected parliament humiliates Ministers who would like to stop live animal exports for veal consumption but are powerless to act without the permission of all EU governments. The Single European Act of 1986 removed the UK's veto in a large number of areas where national interests are subjugated to EU law. Moreover, we are now told that a single currency and EMU is almost a *fait accompli,* since other countries will go ahead anyway and drag us in their wake, whilst the 1991

Maastricht Treaty envisages the replacement of monetary policies designed to achieve national objectives by an EU-wide policy set by an un-elected independent European Central Bank (ECB).

If, however, we have been misled and the economic consequences of EU membership are far from the rosy picture painted by Euro-apologists, how should the UK respond to pressure for further integration which continues even after the 1992 ERM debacle? Is John Major right, that Britain's national interest is best pursued by remaining at the 'heart of Europe', of even an integrationist and un-democratic Europe? Is Tony Blair correct that "no sane person thinks that pulling out of Europe altogether would be in Britain's best interests"? Clearly there are *always* alternatives which can be followed, but instead of analysing each possibility to determine action, many influential opinion leaders merely *assume* that we cannot follow a more independent strategy on an issue which goes to the heart of what kind of country Britain wants to be. Such a lack of confidence in our ability to manage our own affairs must be replaced by a programme whose primary objective is to further the democratic rights and the prosperity of UK citizens. This pamphlet is written as a contribution to the development of that programme.

CHAPTER I

The Past Cost of EU Membership to the UK

The finance of the country is ultimately associated with the liberties of the country. It is a powerful leverage by which English liberty has been gradually aquired. If the House of Commons by any possibility lose the power of the control of the grants of pubic money, depend upon it, your very liberty will be worth very little in comparison.

William E. Gladstone, 1891

EU membership resulted in large net costs being imposed upon the UK economy whilst simultaneously limiting the number of policy tools the government can use to counteract these negative tendencies. Membership burdened the UK with a substantial balance of payments cost, net contributions to the EU budget and the expensive Common Agricultural Policy (CAP). Policy options were narrowed by the enforced abandonment of capital controls and monetary policy restricted to maintaining external balance during membership of the Exchange Rate Mechanism (ERM) rather than pursuing domestic goals of employment, stable prices and economic growth. Subsidies and other elements of an active industrial policy are also rejected as legitimate options for restructuring of industry by EU rules. Furthermore, attempting to meet the Maastricht Treaty's convergence criteria constrains to an unprecedented degree the ability of a democratically elected government to develop an economic programme through its budgetary policy.

BALANCE OF TRADE

The 1971 White Paper (Cmnd. 4715), which laid the ground for UK membership of the EU, argued that accession would produce beneficial economic effects because:

> *"the government is convinced that our economy will be stronger and our industries and people more prosperous if we join the European Communities than if we remain outside them ... improvements in efficiency and competitive power should enable the UK to meet the balance of payments cost of entry as they gradually build up ... the advantages will far outweigh the costs, provided we seize the opportunities of the far wider home market now open to us."*

However, these predictions have been proved to be nothing more than unrealistic hopes not subsequently realised. Indeed, the relative decline of British manufacturing has not only continued but accelerated. UK growth has been constrained by its persistent balance of payments deficit with the EU, which choked-off periods of expansion and forced deflationary policies upon unwilling governments to restore trade equilibrium. Deflation lowers economic growth, increases unemployment and hampers long-term competitiveness, thus exacerbating future difficulties. Since the UK generally enjoys a trading surplus with the rest of the world, it is the EU countries, and especially Germany, which are the cause of the UK's problems. In short, the economic promise offered by EC membership proved to be a mirage.

Membership of the EU customs union forced the UK government to remove tariffs on trade between member states, thus exposing domestic manufacturing industry to stiffer competition, whilst imposing a common external tariff on trade with all other countries. This discriminates against some of the world's poorest countries by encouraging the purchase of goods from less efficient EU producers, thereby reallocating resources *away* from the most efficient producers and *reducing* the economic welfare assumed to arise from free trade. Therefore, a customs union such as the EU does not necessarily imply a move towards freer trade, so that the gains assumed to flow from it do not necessarily accrue. For the UK, previously a relatively free trader, the beneficial resource reallocation imposed by incorporation within the EU failed to outweigh the disadvantages. The initial effect of this change in trade regime was a sharp deterioration in the UK balance of trade in manufactures with EU countries, from a £385 million surplus in 1970 to a deficit of £8,500 million by 1990. Between 1973 and 1977, the UK lost the equivalent of 6% of real national income due to this worsening trade performance, whilst the UK's visible cumulative trade deficit with other EU states during the whole period of membership is £87 billion, equivalent to £145 billion at today's prices. This is a staggering amount of money to be drained from the UK economy, which led to a depreciation in the value of sterling, thus loading higher living costs onto UK consumers and generating an inflationary price-income spiral.

Imports from the EU only increased UK unemployment by approximately 22,734 per year prior to EU membership (between 1960 and 1972), but after accession in 1973 the average annual unemployment caused by EU import penetration leapt to around 200,000 per year. These estimates suggest a staggering total of 3.4 million jobs lost over the period of EU membership to 1989. Despite a degree of compensatory job creation in the non-manufacturing economy, this still represented a cumulative loss greater than the current unemployment level. Thus, the greater part of the mass unemployment blight suffered in the UK over the past two decades was caused by the higher volume of EU imports, resulting largely from the removal of restrictions within the customs union (Burkitt, Baimbridge & Reed 1992, 60–61). The cost to the exchequer for each unemployed person is estimated to be in excess of £9,000 (Berry, Kitson & Michie 1995, 8), so the 3.4 million fall in employment during this period cost the taxpayer approximately £306 billion in today's money. It is therefore trade with the EU, rather than with the rest of the world, that generates the balance of payments constraint upon the UK's capacity for growth and for reducing unemployment.

Despite these enormous social and economic costs of EU membership, many assert that the UK cannot leave the EU because this would reduce UK exports and threaten the influx of direct investment into the country, especially from Japan. Claims that withdrawing from the EU would cost the UK 2.5 million jobs through lost exports neglect the net balance of imports and exports, which induces an overall export of employment (Burkitt, Baimbridge & Reed 1992, 10). Moreover, foreign investment is undertaken in the UK for a variety of reasons, including the fact that English is the foreign language that the Japanese mostly speak. The Japanese themselves have emphasised their need for a commitment to a competitive exchange rate that makes Japanese exports from their UK base cheaper. For example, Ms Haruko Fukuda, vice Chairperson of the Nikko (Europe) division of the international banking group, stated that Japanese companies with plants in the UK would prefer the UK to remain outside the single currency in order to benefit from a competitive exchange rate (Chatham House conference, 29 March 1995, London).

More importantly, Euro-enthusiasts assume that the only viable economic future for a medium-sized nation like the UK, is to join a larger trading bloc. However, current trade statistics demonstrate that this is a naive assumption. The UK undertakes a considerable proportion of its international trade with EU member states, but they do not account for a majority of British trade. After two decades within the EU, the UK's economy is considerably less orientated towards EU trade than other member countries. Including visible and invisible trade, the EU accounts for less than half of UK exports and imports, whilst in 1993 only 18% of UK manufacturing industry's sales (28% of exports) were purchased by EU members. Exports to the Far East have grown almost twice as quickly as those to EU member states between 1987 and 1994, whilst trade with certain countries in that area increased remarkably (Table 1.1). Clearly UK companies do not expect further European integration to offer equal returns to match investment in the fastest growing areas of the world.

Table 1.1

Growth in Exports to four Far Eastern Countries, 1987–1995 (£m)

Year	China	Thailand	Singapore	Philippines
1987	36.1	17.9	55.3	9.9
1989	36.3	37.1	67.2	11.9
1994	960.6	60.6	143.6	28.9
1995	1176.2	69.4	157.3	40.8
real % change	2201.7%	174.1%	112.5%	191.8%

Source: OECD Monthly Statistics of Foreign Trade, OECD, Paris, various editions 1987 to 1995
[Note: figures for 1995 are based upon annualised half yearly figures – £1=$1.57]

EU BUDGET

The EU budget is financed through four means; agricultural levies, customs duties, a set proportion of VAT receipts on a nationally harmonised basket of goods and services, and a calculation based upon the size of each nation's GDP. These four 'own resources' contributed 3%, 18%, 52% and 27% of EU total resources in 1994 respectively. The VAT element is a particular problem for the UK, since historically higher private consumption rates than the EU average lead to the payment of relatively high amounts to the EU according to the VAT rule. Moreover, VAT-exempt goods are included in this calculation by adding in the proportion of VAT which would be paid if they were not zero-rated.

In 1994–5 the UK's gross contribution to the EU budget was estimated to be £8.3 billion. After the abatement Mrs Thatcher negotiated at Fontainebleau in 1984 (which runs until 1999) and receipts from various EU programmes, the UK's net contribution to the EU budget is expected to be £2.45 billion. The

Table 1.2

Net Contributions to the 1993 EU Budget (£m);

Country	Contributions	Money Received	Net Contribution Total	Net Contribution Per capita
Belgium	1,864	1,911	-46	-5
Denmark	939	1,233	-293	-57
Germany	14,851	5,641	9,210	113
Greece	787	4,008	-3,220	-311
Spain	4,027	6,433	-2,406	-62
France	8,988	8,195	794	14
Ireland	442	2,288	-1,847	-519
Italy	7,991	6,804	1,188	21
Luxembourg	130	278	-148	-375
Netherlands	3,138	2,105	1,033	68
Portugal	708	2,661	-1,953	-209
UK	5,937	3,504	2,433	42
TOTAL	49,804	45,060	4,744	14

Source: Miller & Dyson 1994

Fontainebleau rebate is in fact a double-edged phenomenon; it lowers Britain's fiscal burden, but can be constantly threatened as a bargaining weapon. Its existence, even to 1999, is not guaranteed. In 1995–6 the net UK payment is forecast to be £3.46 billion. Even in 1993 the net EU budgetary cost to every UK family was around £145 annually. Even though the UK was the eighth-wealthiest of the then twelve EU member states, it was the second highest contributor to EU funds in absolute terms and the third largest per capita. In per capita terms, the UK is the third largest contributor, after Germany and the Netherlands (Table 1.2). According to this method of calculation, the UK's net payments to the EU in 1993 accounted for £42 for every man, woman and child per annum (Miller & Dyson 1994).

The Commission argues that switching budget finance from VAT receipts towards a greater correlation with a country's GDP will lead to France, Netherlands, Sweden and Austria all paying more into the budget than the UK. However, the success France in particular has enjoyed in opposing greater liberalisation of the Common Agricultural Policy in its own self-interest may mean that such a redistribution in contribution rates is hard to achieve in practice. Moreover, the EU budget increased by 55% over the last 5 years, substantially above the rate of inflation. Over a longer period from 1979 to 1994, EU expenditure rose by an average 11.7% per annum whilst average inflation across the whole EU was only 6.6%. This represents a substantial, consistent real increase in EU resources at a time when national governments were attempting to restrain their budgets. By 1996/7 the 23 years of EU membership will have cost the UK an estimated £30 billion in net budget contributions at current prices.

The Edinburgh Agreement in 1992 allowed EU resources to grow from 1.15% of EU GNP in 1988 and 1.2% in 1993 to 1.27% in 1999. The Commission had requested 1.37%, demonstrating that their ambitions were more grandiose than member states' purse strings. At constant 1992 prices, EU resources will increase from 69.2 billion ECU in 1993 to 84.1 billion ECU in 1999. Breaking down this bill, the 14,918 Commission employees cost £579.6 million in 1994. The European Parliament cost £486.3 million in 1993, estimated to rise to £502.8 million by 1995, a 3.4% increase. Because of the European Parliament's split sites, it needs multiple buildings to conduct its limited business. It rents five buildings in Strasbourg (with one currently under construction), five in Luxembourg and nine in Brussels, with a combined total annual cost of £58.1 million once the new building is occupied.

The UK contributes approximately 12% (without the Fontainebleau abatement it would be 17%) of the EU's resources and in return receives receipts around 8% of total EU expenditure. Thus the UK contributes 4% net of the EU's total resources. If Britain's net payments to the EU stopped immediately, the Chancellor could eliminate the unpopular imposition of VAT on gas and

7

electricity bills or cut 1½p off the standard rate of income tax without increasing the public sector borrowing requirement.

The Edinburgh Agreement marked an attempt to switch EU spending away from agricultural support towards structural actions to ameliorate poverty and the negative effects of European integration within member countries. It is estimated that structural operations will increase between 1993 and 1999 by 41%, with the Cohesion Fund rising by 73% and External Action (largely providing assistance to Eastern European states) by 42%. Nonetheless agricultural spending is still expected to absorb at least 46% of EU expenditure by the turn of the century. The UK receives relatively little from agricultural support due to its efficient production and greater concentration on non-agricultural sectors. Moreover, the areas of greatest increases in EU expenditure, namely external support and the Cohesion Fund, by definition exclude the UK. The Cohesion Fund, for example, is intended to benefit only the poorest members which currently means Spain, Portugal, Greece and Ireland. Consequently, Britain is being asked to pay more to bribe the Mediterranean states and Ireland to support a Maastricht Treaty which is against its national interests.

The UK's relatively large contributions to the EU budget are even harder to bear when the Court of Auditors, the Commission's own financial watchdog, has made the "conservative estimate" that an incredible 10% of the EU's entire budget, some £5–6 billion, is wasted every year through fraud (Lockwood 1994). In a 500 page report, which catalogues waste and fraud on a grand scale, the Court of Auditors (1995) repeat many criticisms first made in 1983 and yet still not resolved. With this wasted money, the EU could either have built a space station, two channel tunnel rail links, fifty hospitals, run a major peacekeeping operation, or a charity the size of Oxfam for half a century!

THE COMMON AGRICULTURAL POLICY

One of the defining moments of British economic and political history occurred in 1846 when Parliament abolished the Corn Laws which protected domestic farmers from imports of foreign grain for over two centuries. It enabled the UK labour force to save money on cheaper food, which could be spent on consumer goods without raising labour costs. This virtuous circle of specialisation in the production of a nation's most efficient goods and services facilitating an optimum allocation of resources was to the advantage of consumers who could buy cheap food, firms whose labour costs were not driven up by high food prices, and food-producing foreign nations who had access to a free market in which to sell their goods and buy British manufactured goods in return (Burkitt & Baimbridge 1990).

The Common Agricultural Policy (CAP) destroyed this beneficial process. By causing a substantial increase in food prices, the cost of living rose for UK consumers and workers, accelerating inflation and generating demands for higher wages and social payments. Consequently UK labour costs increased which reduced industrial competitiveness. Because the UK has traditionally been a net importer of foodstuffs and exporter of manufactured goods, the decline in competitiveness and increased food import prices further burdened the balance of payments. Thus the UK became a net EU budget contributor to sustain the CAP which damages its economic viability since a worsening balance of payments reduces the scope of the UK economy to expand before a trade deficit requires government to introduce deflationary policies. These restore a trade balance at the cost of higher unemployment, reductions in economic growth and a long term loss of industrial competitiveness. CAP prices were first imposed in 1973, and subsequently contributed to the substantial inflation experienced in Britain during the second half of the 1970s.

Throughout the 1980s EU food prices were on average 70% higher than on the world market (Burkitt, Baimbridge & Reed 1992, 14). Ironically one of CAP's aims enshrined in the Treaty of

Rome was the provision of reasonably priced foodstuffs! According to a recent National Consumer Council (1995) estimate in September 1995, the CAP costs an average UK family (i.e. 2 adults and 2 children) £20 in higher weekly bills than if food was bought on world markets. This can be compared to an average 1994 household's (i.e. average 2.4 individuals) weekly food bill of £50.43 (CSO 1995). Total CAP agricultural support, including taxpayers' contribution to farming via the EU budget and the cost of destroying surplus produce, is estimated to cost the average British family £28 per week (Booker 1994). Combining the effect of the higher prices caused by the CAP, and the cost to the taxpayer to keep the system going, the average cost to the British employee is one quarter the size of their entire income tax and social security contributions. The cost to non-farm EU households was estimated at around £830 per year in 1990, and growing to £1,150 by the turn of the century (*The Economist* 12/12/1992). Indeed the burden the CAP imposed upon families is so great that, if they had saved their contributions to the CAP during the 1980s, they would on average possess sufficient funds to buy several acres of UK farmland and established their own subsistence farm!

Whilst the CAP doubles farmers' incomes over their level if they sold produce at world prices, it achieves this objective inefficiently. For every £100 which farmers receive through the system, consumers and taxpayers contribute £160. Moreover, the bulk of these subsidies do not help to increase the wages of lowly paid agricultural workers. A world-wide study estimated that 50% of farm subsidies are invested in additional production, 45.2% are taken as profits and a mere 4.8% are used to increase the pay of agricultural labour (Johnson 1991). Another study by Anderson & Tyers (1993) found that agricultural support leads to a 37% waste of resources as food production is stimulated at inefficient locations or with relatively expensive combination of land, labour, capital and chemical fertilisers. Indeed, abolishing such subsidies would reduce the incidence of environmental problems caused by farming; with less chemicals used than at present, fewer compensatory measures, such as filtering the water supply in farming areas, are required.

The impact of the CAP resembles that of agricultural support in Adam Smith's day, when the Corn Laws were at their peak, he wrote:

> "... the interest of the consumer is almost constantly sacrificed to that of the producer; [the system] seems to consider production, and not consumption, as the ... object of all industry and commerce."

> (*The Economist* 12/12/1992)

It is time the balance was again redressed.

Since public expenditure to support agricultural prices could be more efficiently spent elsewhere, the CAP involves a substantial hidden opportunity cost. An OECD study estimated that complete liberalisation of world agricultural support and investment of the resources saved in more efficient production would increase world wealth by £325 billion per year. European GDP was believed to be 2.5% below what it could be if agricultural liberalisation replaced the CAP. Moreover, the UK would benefit more than other EU member states because its net loss from the CAP is greater. Consequently, abolition would release proportionally more resources for more efficient investment in UK manufacturing industry or financial services. However, even if the UK merely gained the average estimate for the whole of the EU, a 2.5% increase in GDP would net £16.7 billion at 1994 prices, which is equivalent in scale to half of the entire annual health budget. Since economic growth is cumulative, this increase becomes more significant over time.

Since the veto system applies to CAP expenditure, it is unlikely that significant reform will occur, since at least France, Denmark, Ireland and the Netherlands benefit from the existing system. The struggle to achieve the latest GATT agreement, and the manoeuvring by France and others to dilute proposed savings, indicates the difficulty of transforming the system into one that benefits consumers. The only realistic possibility of reform appears to lie in the financial impact on EU membership of enlargement to Eastern Europe (see Chapter V). The Treasury estimates the cost of EU enlargement for the UK to be around

£6 billion per year in CAP contributions alone, which is equivalent to adding 3p to the standard rate of income tax. It is often assumed that the cost for current EU members will lead to a substantial pruning of CAP expenditure. However, it might equally result in those countries who most benefit from CAP expenditure blocking new entrants until they receive compensatory payments, which will further disadvantage the UK.

THE COMMON FISHERIES POLICY

The Common Fisheries Policy (CFP) is a notorious example of how the UK gave away control of its resources after EU accession. Immediately prior to Britain's entry, the six original members, without sanction from the Treaty of Rome, devised the CFP as a way of gaining access to the 60–80% of fish in European waters which lay within the British territorial limit. In his eagerness to enter the Community, Edward Heath surprisingly agreed to this self-interested manoeuvre, accepting fish to be a 'common European resource' which anyone could catch anywhere in the Community. By accepting this, he gave away part of UK citizens' birthright and sowed the seeds for the decline of the UK fishing industry. Whilst the number of fish consumed in 1988 was approximately equal to the level in 1971, the proportion provided by UK vessels fell over the period from over 85% to only 61%, with imports rising three-fold (Sleath 1995, 20). As the transitory agreement has recently expired, the UK had to negotiate hard to prevent more than 40 Spanish boats from fishing in the 100,000 square mile 'Irish Box' at any one time. Spain possesses the world's largest fishing fleet but enjoys relatively few waters of its own, so that inevitably it sought to take advantage of the CFP to fish intensively in UK waters.

Over-fishing is the consequence of limited grounds supporting an influx of new fleets, embodying improved technology to enable larger catches to be landed. The EU response to this plundering of a scarce natural resource was not to re-establish national fishing rights, but to impose in 1983 a system of quotas or "total allowable catches", to restrict the numbers of fish which can be landed in a year. As each fishing vessel receives its share of the quota, the right for non-UK vessels to fish in UK territorial waters is enshrined. However, quotas only relate to the landing of certain categories of fish. They result in fishermen throwing thousands of tons of dead fish back into the sea before arriving at port to avoid infringing the quota, which does little to protect the smaller fish needed to sustain future stocks. Scientists estimate that in some EU waters, the scale of fraudulent catches is as high as 10–20%, with a further 40% of the catch species being discarded.

The Save Britain's Fish campaign argues that an efficient conservation strategy should be introduced instead of the quota failure, based upon the widespread utilisation of new technology which can control the size and species of fish caught in trawler nets. This technology is utilised by the Norwegian and Canadian governments but is steadfastly rejected by the EU. However, the real possibility is that the supply of cod, haddock and many other fish species could expire in less than a generation, unless intelligent changes are instituted towards fish conservation policy. This must concern not only fishermen, who rely upon healthy and successfully managed stocks to provide their living, but also the UK government's environmental advisors on the panel established to implement the Rio Earth Summit Commitments, headed by Sir Crispin Tickell. However, in view of the failings of the present CFP, the reluctance of the EU to make the necessary changes and the relatively short time period this must take to minimise further losses of fish stocks, it appears inevitable that the UK must withdraw from the CFP to effectively protect remaining fish stocks.

Enforcement of the CFP is the responsibility of the shore authorities from which the fishing vessels originate. They possess little interest in enforcing quotas or in discovering where the fish were caught. Indeed, were they to redouble their efforts to monitor the CFP more effectively, methods of avoidance are relatively easy and reliably ascertaining where fish were caught is almost impossible for a land-based authority. This gaping hole in the CFP could only be closed by a massive enforcement campaign at sea. However, other EU members, particularly Spain, would then complain of Royal Navy harassment! Such problems would intensify with enlargement as countries such as Poland, Bulgaria and the Baltic states, who possess large fishing fleets, can only be incorporated within the CFP at the expense of Britain.

The CFP has been an unmitigated disaster for UK fishermen and UK consumers, who have endured price rises as a result of restricted supply and lower utilisation of vessel capacity. However, the acceptance of fish as a common European resource might have one further, even more damaging consequence. If fish is treated as a common resource, oil and natural gas could be similarly regarded. The logic is compelling and such an enlargement of EU authority would be in the direct interest of all EU nations apart from the UK and the Netherlands. Since oil provided a large slice of government revenue throughout the 1980s and boosted UK exports significantly, any loss of this national resource would detrimentally affect the UK's economy. Whilst the CFP sets a precedent for treating sea-bound national resources as common, the threat to oil and gas remains. It is crucial the UK government refuses any suggestion to take away its control over its North Sea oil and gas production and revenues.

VALUE ADDED TAX

The power to raise taxation is one of the cornerstones of any elected assembly, whether at local or national level. Without the ability to control the flow of revenue, a democratic body is fatally weakened when determining expenditure and the general balance of macroeconomic policy. The slogan of 'no taxation without representation' enabled the creation and development of many parliaments. Taxing people who have no opportunity to challenge or change tax methods and levels historically proved unpopular, providing the impetus for the Peasants' Revolt of 1381 and the American War of Independence. Therefore, the stealth by which the EU has appropriated national governments' determination of VAT rates is both damaging to democracy and ultimately self-destructive.

The EU Commission believes tax harmonisation to be essential, in the long run, for the single market to work efficiently.

Harmonisation eventually implies identical tax regimes, including all capital, income, consumption and social insurance tax rates. However, aiming to achieve its objectives through an incremental process, the EU has initially focused upon indirect taxation and excise duties. It wants to eliminate zero rating for goods and services and install only two VAT bands; a standard rate between 14–20% and a reduced rate between 4–9%. If zero rating was eliminated in the UK, amongst those areas affected would be the following; books and newspapers (with spill-over effects upon educational provision and the general literacy of the population), public transport (at a time when environmental pressures demand an expanded, inexpensive public transportation system), food (already expensive due to the CAP) and children's clothes (inequitable since it bears proportionally more upon the poor). The elderly, who are a growing proportion of the community, and the poorest members of society will lose most if zero rating is abandoned, since a higher proportion of their incomes are spent upon these items. The end result would be regressive, since income would be distributed from the less well off to the relatively affluent members of the community. Meanwhile, the Commission focuses upon VAT harmonisation, whilst ignoring large-scale smuggling of alcohol and cigarettes.

Whether the UK can retain its ability to zero rate selected goods in the long-term is doubtful if the track record of accommodation to the EU on matters of self interest is noted. However, one current EU rule which has made its mark is that, once zero rating has been removed on a particular good or service, it can never be re-imposed. The sensitive issue of VAT on domestic fuel created considerable opposition to a tax perceived to be unfair and unnecessary. However, despite unease amongst many in all parties, once the non-zero rate was introduced, EU rules forbid any government, even one elected on the basis of a specific manifesto commitment, to re-introduce zero rating. UK citizens are thus prevented from exercising their democratic rights of changing taxation. Thus, by introducing a ratchet effect, whereby a decision once imposed by an unelected body can never be reversed, the EU flouts the democratic principle that the voters are able to alter previous policies. Pledges made in the 1975 referendum have already been broken by giving the EU the right to determine, at least partially, UK tax rates. Opinion polls demonstrate that many voters feel that the contract to which they assented has been broken.

LOSS OF SELF-GOVERNMENT

The Maastricht Treaty committed the EU to evolve towards eventual political, economic and monetary union, which would turn Parliament at Westminster into a mere assembly rubber stamping 'union' legislation and acting as a peripheral local authority, dealing with a remote centralised bureaucracy operating hundreds of miles away. However, even before this Treaty was enacted, the ability of the UK Parliament to legislate in the interests of its citizens was heavily circumscribed. Technical and safety standards, for example, are supposed to become uniform to prevent non-tariff barriers frustrating free trade within the single market. Even though British standards are often recognised as amongst the best in the world, the UK holds only one in five of the positions on the secretariat servicing the technical committees of the European Standardisation Committee, meaning it is likely that UK standards will often have to be changed, and in many cases, lowered.

More generally, EU membership decisively limits the scope for self-government previously enjoyed by the UK. Whilst Section 2(2) of the 1972 European Communities Act remains on the statute book, any UK government will be compelled by British courts to reverse policies which conflict with EU law. For instance, the European Court ruled that differential pension ages were discriminatory and the UK government had to obey this verdict, with the result that women must work five years longer before receiving a full state pension. Moreover, on matters of great public interest, such as the dispute over shipping live animals to the Continent, the UK government cannot pass legislation which an overwhelming majority of its citizens would welcome because of the primacy of EU law. Instead, UK

Ministers are humiliated as they agonise in public about what they would like to do if only they had the power to do it. Thus they are reduced to resembling a lower functionary within a large organisation rather than a democratically accountable Minister charged with pursuing the national interest.

THE EU AND QMV

The EU is unlike most other international organisations where unanimity is required because many policies can be implemented on the basis of a qualified voting majority (QMV) amongst member states. The main EU decision-making and legislative body is the Council of Ministers, which comprises Ministers from national governments supported by permanent bureaucrats based in Brussels. In the early years of the European integration process, decisions were taken unanimously. However, agricultural decisions, which were then (as now) the dominant area of EU spending, quickly became subject to majority voting, which was enshrined in the 1957 Treaty of Rome (Hopkins 1995, 32). Later, a dispute between France and the EU over decision taking was resolved in the 1966 Luxembourg Compromise, which stated that where important interests of one or more member nations are involved a solution which all could accept should be pursued. The French added an addendum stating that, if an important interest was at stake, discussion must continue until unanimous agreement was achieved. However, this decision was weakened during following years, in that the precise basis upon which member states are allowed to claim vital interests, and thereby exercise their veto, is largely determined by other member states. Such momentum was enshrined in legislation by the 1986 Single European Act, which introduced qualified majority voting in most areas of the internal market.

Qualified majority voting requires a 70% majority in favour of a proposal rather than a simple majority. Prior to the enlargement of the EU to 15 nations, the 30% blocking minority meant 23 votes out of the 76 votes available; after enlargement this has risen to 26 votes out of a total 87. It means that the UK would have to form alliances with at least two other member states to block legislation which is not in its national interest. Since the UK's trading profile is significantly different from that of most other member states, and its economic requirements are correspondingly different from the prescriptions of economic orthodoxy currently pervading the EU, this loss of national self-governance will adversely affect Britain.

A report co-written by Niels Ersboll, until last year the secretary-general of the European Council, and Peter Ludlow of the Centre for European Policy Studies (a leading Brussels think-tank) argues that the EU should extend majority voting to foreign and security policy (Ersboll & Ludlow 1995). It also states that all countries which opt out of EU policies, or engage in "unacceptable behaviour" which destabilises the union, should face sanctions and be treated as a second class member. This controversial suggestion, coming from individuals of influence within the EU élite, would include punishing sustained opposition to further EU integration and would have covered the UK's unilateral devaluation in 1992. Should such an unwarranted suggestion be adopted by the EU Commission, it would effectively reduce any nation's ability to disagree with the prevailing wisdom espoused by the EU's civil service and the dominant French-German axis. They would be treated as pariahs with no right to hold contrary opinions, never mind utilise their democratic rights to actively oppose them. The possibility is not remote. The German Finance Minister, Theo Weigell, with the support of the Bundesbank, recently called for fines upon countries who do not conform to the Maastricht convergence criteria, in an endeavour to reassure domestic public opinion about the stability of any future single currency.

The current voting system disproportionally favours the smaller EU nations at the expense of the larger. To make this system fairer, voting patterns need to reflect population sizes. This would lead to the UK's share of voting power rising from its present 11.5% to 15.7%, approximately the same as France and Italy, whilst Germany would receive 22.0% of the total votes. The smaller nations would generally have their voting power reduced

Table 1.3
Alternative Scenarios for the Allocation of
Votes in the Council of Ministers

Member State		Current Votes	Allocation Share (%)	Option One (Population)		Option Two (Budget)	
				Votes	Share	Votes	Share
Belgium		5	5.7	27	2.7	18	3.6
Denmark		3	3.4	14	1.4	8	1.6
France		10	11.5	155	15.7	85	17.1
Germany		10	11.5	217	22.0	138	27.7
Greece		5	5.7	27	2.7	6	1.2
Ireland		3	3.4	9	0.9	4	0.8
Italy		10	11.5	153	15.5	67	13.4
Luxembourg		2	2.3	1	0.1	1	0.2
Netherlands		5	5.7	41	4.1	29	5.8
Portugal		5	5.7	26	2.6	7	1.4
Spain		8	9.2	105	10.6	39	7.8
UK		10	11.5	155	15.7	54	10.8
Austria		4	4.6	21	2.1	17	3.4
Finland		3	3.4	14	1.4	9	1.8
Sweden		4	4.6	23	2.3	16	3.2
Total		87		988		498	
Blocking	30%	26		296		149	
Minority	40%	35		395		199	
Required	50%	44		494		249	

Source: Baimbridge & Burkitt 1995a

to half or one-third of its present value, although Luxembourg would suffer the most with its voting share falling from a current 3.3% to only 0.1% in the future (Table 1.3 – option one).

A second alternative to the present voting mechanism is to base the number of votes each member state receives upon the size of its contribution to the EU budget (Table 1.3 – option two). The consequence of this reform would be to redistribute voting power towards the pay-masters of the EU and consequently result in expenditure being more stringently reviewed. Under this scenario, Germany's share of the votes rises to 27.7%, which is very close to reaching the 30% blocking majority figure; consequently, if its relative contribution to the EU budget increases, it would possess an absolute veto on EU expenditure.

In view of Denmark's suspicion that political union will cause larger nations to dominate smaller member states, any such change would be contentious. Sweden has stated that it will strenuously oppose any attempt by larger nations to strengthen their hold on levers of power within the EU. However, even after a change based upon population, the UK would possess only half the voting power necessary to block unfavourable legislation. Thus, even a fairer voting system would not prevent the UK's essential interests from being ignored by an integrationist EU qualified majority.

CHAPTER II

Current Costs of the EU

Whilst the EU has imposed substantial historical costs on Britain, more recent events have, and are still, damaging its economy. The two most obvious examples are the ERM debacle and the stringent terms set out in the Maastricht Treaty for economic and monetary convergence.

THE COST OF ERM MEMBERSHIP

The European Exchange Rate Mechanism (ERM) was instigated by Giscard d'Estaing and Helmut Schmidt in 1979, as part of the European Monetary System (EMS). It is based upon the European Currency Unit (ECU) which is a composite of member countries' currencies. Bilateral rates for each participating currency are calculated against all others and measured against the central ECU rate. Each currency is fixed within a band (currently varying between 2.25% and 15%), which defines the limit within which it is allowed to fluctuate relative to other member currencies. If a currency falls to the floor of its band, the relevant government is committed to prevent the band being breached by intervening in financial markets to support its currency; it can apply for loans from fellow participants to sustain this intervention. The repayment terms of such loans are subject to a strict timetable, so that sustained pressure on a currency leaves the country with little alternative to deflating its economy to relieve the pressure and ensure ERM rules are adhered to.

The ERM was designed to provide exchange rate stability through mutual co-operation between participating countries' central banks to safeguard their currencies against short term speculation and remove uncertainty from trade. The deutschmark acts as the anchor for the system and the rationale for Germany to establish this system was to keep the value of its currency down against the dollar at the expense of other EU currencies (Burkitt,

Baimbridge & Mills 1993, 4). However, despite frequent realignments within the system during its first four years, after 1983 the ERM reduced currency volatility at the cost of preventing realignments which are necessary to reflect a country's changing long-term competitive position.

The exchange rate between two countries is a price, just like any other. Its correct level at any particular time is that which enables an economy to combine full employment of productive resources with a simultaneous approximate balance of payments equilibrium. A higher exchange rate causes overseas trade deficits and unemployment, whilst a lower one leads to an excessive build up of foreign currency reserves and stimulates domestic inflationary pressures. Thus, every nation must retain the ability to adjust the external value of its currency; to fix it within narrow, rigid limits courts disaster. The argument that devaluation is always self-defeating, since it increases inflation thereby eliminating any competitive advantage secured by lowering the exchange rate, does not reflect the available evidence. In 1931 and 1949 UK devaluation boosted exports, growth and production without leading to an inflationary spiral. Moreover, the current UK economic improvement clearly dates from the UK being forced out of the ERM and the consequent resulting approximate 10% devaluation. Exports and the growth rate have increased whilst unemployment has fallen, without a simultaneous inflationary surge undermining these achievements. Indeed, the main factor causing concern about the long-term sustainability of the recovery is not the threat of inflation, but rather the reluctance of UK manufacturing industry to use the higher profits to invest in future production. In these circumstances, sterling will need to fall further if a substantial export-led boom is to occur.

Since ERM adjustments are agreed unanimously, members can veto the attempts of another participating country to adjust its exchange rate to maintain international competitiveness. Moreover, each country benefits from another's loss of competitiveness, at least in the short term, so that the threat of a veto is strong. Thus, in the absence of the ability to devalue, a country must deflate its economy to remain within the ERM bands it has been allocated, with resulting higher unemployment, lower growth and a deterioration in its long term competitive position.

Whilst the ERM has operated largely to Germany's benefit by enlisting other EU countries to keep the deutschmark's value competitively low against non-EU currencies, this achievement has been at the expense of the rest of the participants. Apart from Japan, France had the fastest growth rate amongst the major OECD countries during the 1960s and 1970s, averaging 1% higher growth than Germany. However, after entry into the ERM and the 1983 'Fortress Franc' policy that refused to devalue despite an increasingly un-competitive currency, the French economy was placed within an ever-tightening straitjacket. Whilst French inflation converged towards that of Germany, French output did not expanded sufficiently to prevent unemployment from steadily rising to above 12% of the labour force.

Unencumbered by fixed parities between 1985 and 1988, Britain let sterling depreciate and reaped the benefits in terms of higher economic growth and falling unemployment. However, this superior position was cast aside to join the ERM. Membership was sought partly due to political pressures from leading figures amongst the cabinet, including Howe, Hurd and Lawson, who wanted to pursue closer European integration, and partly to restore the faith of the financial markets in the government's anti-inflationary credentials after the uncontrolled price rises caused by liberalisation of UK capital markets. The UK joined the ERM in October 1990 at a fixed central parity of 2.95 deutschmarks to the pound, a rate intended to put immediate pressure upon the UK economy to reduce inflation rather than institutionalising a competitive exchange rate. Unsurprisingly, this chosen rate, and ERM membership itself, proved to be a big mistake.

During the period of ERM membership (October 1990–September 1992), the UK economy fell into a deep recession. In terms of GDP volume, the economy shrunk by 3.86%. At the same time, unemployment rose by 1.2 million to 2.85 million, on official government figures, and by 1.3 million (to 3.99 million) if numbers were calculated on the same statistical basis as they were in 1979.[†] Whilst it is very difficult to estimate the extent to which these negative events were due solely to ERM membership and which were due to other circumstances, it is nevertheless worth noting two points. First, immediately prior to ERM membership, UK growth was averaging about 2% per year and the same immediately afterwards, whilst membership coincided with 6 out of 8 quarters of economic decline. Unemployment prior to ERM membership stood at 5.5% whilst after sterling left the ERM unemployment began to fall consistently again. The clear pattern is slightly confused because of the time lag experienced between more expansive economic policy and unemployment actually beginning to fall. Thus, even though other forces influenced economic developments, the ERM coincided with a specific period of decline and rapidly rising unemployment, whilst periods immediately before and after membership displayed improved performance. Moreover, whilst international factors may have negatively affected the UK between 1990 and 1992, ERM membership constrained the UK from responding by a more expansive economic policy and thereby further depressed the economy.

When estimating the burden of ERM membership, a 1.2 million increase in those unemployed and claiming benefit costs the taxpayer a total of £10.8 billion according to the Treasury estimate that the average unemployed person loses the state £9,000 in terms of benefits paid and tax forgone. This sum is equivalent to 1.8% of 1992 UK GDP. The 3.9% fall in GDP during ERM membership amounts to £23.1 billion in 1992 money. Thus, the 'conservative' estimate of the ERM's impact upon the UK is £33.9 billion, reducing its GDP by 5.7%. However, this understates the actual loss the UK suffered through ERM membership, because it normally would be expected to expand along its 2.5% long term growth rate. Therefore, at the end of two years of ERM membership, the UK national income should have been 5.1% higher than it actually was, representing £30.3 billion at 1992 prices. Adding the cost of defending sterling within its ERM

---

† The Unemployment Unit (322 St John Street, London, EC1V 4NT) calculates UK unemployment rates according to the statistical definition used by the government prior to 1979.

parity, variously estimated at between £4 to £15 billion, and the total cost of ERM membership for the UK lies between £68.2 billion and £79.2 billion (11.5% to 13.3% of 1992 UK GDP).

To put all of this into some context, if the UK had not lost a minimum of £68.2 billion by entering the ERM, the UK would not have suffered budget deficits between 1994 and 1996, so that the government would not have needed to raise taxes and cut public spending. Alternatively, the unpopular VAT on fuel would not have been introduced and income tax could have been completely abolished for the 1993–94 tax year, or spending upon the NHS could have been more than doubled for one year, thereby more than resolving under-funding in the health sector. ERM membership, however, ensured that all of these resources were not available for such positive uses and were instead wasted in leaving people on the dole rather than utilising their skills in productive uses to meet peoples' needs. Additionally, crime rates and ill health tend to increase with unemployment, so that the total social cost for society is significantly higher, although less easy to quantify (Berry, Kitson & Michie 1995). ERM membership was therefore a calamity for the UK economy and society, the price of which is still being paid.

The partial collapse of the ERM in the Autumn of 1992 and the Summer of 1993 arose from a fundamental flaw in its construction; it was simultaneously too rigid because it obliged governments to maintain parity rates even after the financial markets had come to believe that they were unsustainable, but not rigid enough because once speculation reached a certain momentum the cost of accommodating such pressure through selling foreign exchange became prohibitive. However, its fundamental failure was its inability to deal with a situation where the anchor economy, West Germany, became preoccupied with its own reunification with East Germany and utilised its monetary policy for domestic priorities. Whilst this was rational in the united Germany's national interests, the operation of the ERM meant that other countries had to raise their interest rates to maintain their external parities, despite their domestic needs requiring a looser monetary policy to prevent recession.

Sterling's ejection from the ERM released the UK economy from persistent deflation and provided the foundation for the non-inflationary growth the economy has subsequently enjoyed. It enabled interest rates and monetary policy to be freed from the sole task of maintaining the exchange rate and contribute towards the growth of the economy. Whilst countries remaining within the ERM have had to maintain high real interest rates to prevent their currencies from falling outside the ERM bands, the UK has been able to benefit from lower rates.

Some of this potential has been utilised, enabling the UK to achieve higher growth and greater reductions in unemployment than many EU countries. However, despite the Sterling Index (covering twenty countries) falling from a high of 103 (1990 = 100) in January 1991 to a more competitive 84.7 in February 1993, the Bank of England subsequently resumed shadowing the deutschmark, forcing sterling to appreciate by 10% by January 1994, since when it has been allowed to decline slightly once again. Interest rates were not lowered in line with inflation, such that the real rate rose to exceed 6% in January 1994 which is a near record during a period of mass unemployment. Without this partial return to an over-valued currency, the UK could have performed more efficiently. Justification for this argument comes from examining the performance of Italy. The lira is currently 20% more competitive than in 1990; as a result Italy has enjoyed one of the fastest growth rates in the last couple of years, whilst its trade balance has moved from deficit into a comfortable surplus.

From Table 2.1, it can be seen that countries within the ERM are severely constrained in their interest rate policy by the need to maintain a real interest rate premium over Germany. In 1993, in particular, Denmark, France and Ireland were forced to maintain real interest rates over twice the level of Germany's despite experiencing low inflation and a trade surplus. Even the Netherlands, which has long shadowed the deutschmark and is effectively within a deutschmark zone, had to maintain real interest rates 34 points higher than Germany in 1993, although this premium declined in 1994. In the wider ERM band, Spain was able to

Table 2.1

Comparing short-term real interest rates with Germany's rates, 1993–1994

EU/ERM relationship	Country	Short-term real interest rates (%)		German index = 100	
		1993	1994	1993	1994
In EU & ERM	Germany	3.2	2.4	100	100
	Netherlands	4.3	2.5	134	104
	Belgium	5.5	3.3	172	138
	Ireland	7.7	3.5	241	146
	France	6.5	4.2	203	175
	Denmark	9.0	4.2	281	175
	Luxembourg	n/a	n/a	n/a	n/a
In EU & ERM	Portugal	n/a	n/a	n/a	n/a
(wide)	Spain	7.2	3.2	225	133
In EU	Austria	3.4	2.1	106	88
but not ERM	UK	4.4	3.0	138	125
	Finland	5.7	4.3	178	179
	Italy	6.0	4.6	188	192
	Sweden	3.8	5.2	119	217
	Greece	n/a	n/a	n/a	n/a
Outside EU	Switzerland	1.5	3.1	47	129
& ERM	Norway	5.0	4.4	156	183

Source: OECD Main Economic Indicators September 1995,18 & 26

maintain a greater range of currency flexibility, despite being one of the weaker EU currencies. It nevertheless had to sustain higher real interest rates than its domestic economic circumstances dictated.

Countries outside the ERM were able to pursue monetary policies aimed at domestic prosperity rather than maintaining their currencies within an arbitrarily defined range of fluctuation against the deutschmark. Austria, in particular, made full use of this policy freedom by maintaining real interest rates only marginally above those of Germany through 1993, and substantially below in 1994. The UK, similarly, responded to its ejection from the ERM by maintaining lower real interest rates than would otherwise have been possible and thereby escaped the worst ravages of the second half of the European recession. Switzerland clearly benefited most in 1993, by reducing real interest rates to 53 points below German rates. Switzerland's comparable 1994 index figure is a little misleading since inflation was only some 0.9% in that year, so that, despite the maintenance of cheap money, its real interest rate rose.

It is important to note, however, that not all countries outside the ERM used their monetary policy freedom to lower real interest rates. Norway and Sweden, for example, were forced to maintain high rates by the near collapse of their respective financial sectors due to an explosion in bad debts resulting from lending on over-inflated property values. Therefore, two conclusions can be drawn. First, ERM membership constrains monetary policy independence by forcing it to maintain external exchange rate parities rather than to achieve domestic goals of growth and employment. This failing is most clearly evident when the economy is entering recession and flexibility is most needed. Secondly, monetary policy independence is a necessary, but not sufficient, prerequisite for lower real interest rates, thereby stimulating economic growth.

In an ever-changing economic environment, the value of the exchange rate which facilitates full employment of domestic resources and an external trade balance will vary. Therefore, it is important for any country to retain control over all national policy instruments to be utilised in pursuit of employment, production and living standards. Speculative fluctuations must be smoothed and the exchange rate managed by a democratically controlled Bank of England to prevent disruption of international trade. However, this does not mean fixed, unchangeable exchange rates as under the ERM. The optimum strategy for international co-operation between central banks on exchange rates requires a combination of maximum short-term stability with maximum long term flexibility.

THE SINGLE INTERNAL MARKET

The Single European Act (SEA), which was adopted by the UK parliament in 1986 and became European Law in 1987, was intended to create a single, unified internal market covering all member states by 31 December 1992. By this date, all formal trade barriers had to be removed, including border controls, whilst ensuring the free movement of capital, people, goods and services between members.

The economic rationale was presented in a report prepared for the EU Commission (Cecchini 1988). Cecchini claimed that consumers would be able to buy cheaper goods after the removal of non-tariff barriers due to increased competition between firms and greater exploitation of economies of scale made possible by a larger market place. The report suggested these benefits would increase EU GDP by 7% and create 5 million new jobs across the Union. This prediction, however, assumes that the potential for greater economies of scale actually exists, and that a single market will not lead to increased monopolisation and consequent retention of monopoly profits. Since non-tariff barriers did not present large obstacles to trade amongst the EU nations before the single internal market (SIM), it was unlikely that their removal would lead to significant economies of scale being achieved which had not already been attained.

In addition, a substantial part of Cecchini's estimated benefits were supposed to come from supply side effects which reduced inflation and balance of payments constraints. Thus increased economic activity would provide increased resources for reflationary government expenditure. To the extent that the loosening of restraints on growth depend upon increasing competition and utilising economies of scale, if these advantages fail to materialise, eventual supply side benefits will be lower than predicted. Furthermore, Cecchini's assumption of concerted reflation amongst EU nations was always implausible and has been superseded by deflationary imperatives demanded by ERM membership and the Maastricht Treaty's fiscal convergence criteria which all members are committed to achieving. Without co-ordinated reflation, a considerable proportion of Cecchini's predicted benefits flowing from the SEA would not materialise (Burkitt & Baimbridge 1991).

Cambridge Econometrics (1990) presented an alternative prediction for the effects of the SIM which was based upon more realistic assumptions than those used by Cecchini and which produced more pessimistic conclusions concerning its impact upon the UK economy. The Cambridge scenario expected the SIM to generate rationalisation of European industry through mergers and concentration of production. These were predicted to result in the loss of 300,000 manufacturing jobs in the UK, possibly offset by a gain of about the same number of service jobs, although the assumed expansion in financial sector employment appears optimistic amidst general job cutting after over-expansion during the 1980s liberalisation. Growth of service employment to compensate for the loss of well paid, skilled manufacturing jobs producing tradable goods may either not appear or be concentrated in low paid, part time sectors.

In addition, the Cambridge model assumes the SIM will exacerbate existing regional differences throughout the EU as a whole and within the UK economy. Thus the greater part of any expansion in growth and employment opportunities resulting from the effects of the single market will disproportionally favour the south east region of the UK, whilst the loss of manufacturing jobs will affect already disadvantaged northern regions. Moreover, since the south eastern region tends to possess relatively tight labour and housing markets, the possible additional demand generated by the SEA might simply lead to inflationary wage and house price pressures rather than generate significant gains in terms of economic growth and employment opportunities.

A study undertaken by the Dutch Central Planning Bureau (Bakhoven 1989), using a world econometric model, predicts significantly more negative results than the Cecchini Report (see Table 2.2). The Dutch model predicts that employment across the

Table 2.2

Medium-term macroeconomic consequences of the SIM: EU and Dutch Central Planning Bureau (CPB) models

Model and Data		CPB	CPB + EU data	EU
Volume of private consumption		2.6	3.2	3.1
Volume of private investments				
in fixed assets:	housing	3.1	4.3	4.7
	other	2.0	2.6	7.0
Volume of goods & services exports		7.6	16.1	10.5
Volume of goods & services imports		7.1	14.7	7.2
Volume of GDP		2.3	3.4	4.5
Labour productivity		2.4	2.3	3.0
Employment		-0.1	0.9	1.5
Rate of capacity utilisation		0.7	1.2	2.5
Financial surplus of government		0.0	1.2	2.2
Balance of payments current account		0.1	0.6	1.0

Source: Bakhoven 1989, 21

EU will fall by some 0.1% over the first six years of SIM operation, meaning approximately 400,000 people will lose their jobs as a direct result of the SIM. Moreover, Cecchini's prediction that the SEA would lead to budget surpluses of some 2.2% of GNP, which could be used to finance a co-ordinated reflationary strategy, is also disputed by the Dutch results which predict no such budget surplus and therefore no additional resources available to finance an employment-generating programme.

Because the single market only fully began operations on 1 January 1993, it is too soon to draw firm conclusions concerning the actual effect it has had on the UK, and test whether the predictions made by the Cecchini Report models were correct. However, the SIM is likely to widen, not diminish, the UK's trade deficit with other EU nations. Employment will be lost in manufacturing. In the absence of the reflationary policies assumed by Cecchini, which are essentially Keynesian measures which could be implemented without the SEA, the final effect on UK growth and employment rates is at best marginal, and at worst will further damage the UK economy at a time when the dynamics of EU membership are increasingly adverse.

INDUSTRY STUDIES

The danger of over-concentration upon the EU single market as the destination for export activity is underlined by examining UK trade developments within specific key industries during the first two years of SIM operations (1st January 1993 to 31st December 1994). The industries examined were those the EU Commission identified as potentially the UK's greatest beneficiaries of the larger market provided by the SIM (EC Commission 1988) and the anticipated greater economies of scale – aircraft, chemicals, dyestuffs, paper products, petroleum products, power generation equipment, synthetic rubber, titanium oxide – and three further important UK industries – computers & automotive machines, metalworking machinery and telecommunications. The results of the industry studies are included in Table 2.3. The percentage change columns allow for the effect of rising prices upon the increased value of trade during this time period so that accurate comparisons can be made in constant 1994 prices.

Four UK industries (aircraft, metalworking machinery, power generation equipment and titanium oxide) experienced substantially *declining* exports in real terms during the first two years of the SIM, with aircraft sales almost halved in real terms. Of those industries recording a real increase in export sales, paper products rose by only a marginal 1.3%. Comparing the development of UK export sales within the SIM against sales to the rest of the world, Table 2.3 clearly shows that only one industry, chemicals, experienced more rapid export growth within the SIM than outside it, and only marginally by 0.6%! Thus, the SIM experience proved extremely disappointing during its establishment and first two years of operation, and demonstrated an inability to

Table 2.3

Real percentage change in UK exports to the EU and the rest of the world between 1992 and 1994

Industry	EU	non-EU	difference
	real % change in exports, 31/12/1992 – 31/12/1994		
Titanium Oxide	-41.4	39.2	-80.6
Aircraft	-47.9	2.6	-50.5
Synthetic Rubber	8.9	56.3	-47.4
Computers Machinery	23.9	68.8	-44.9
Metalworking Machinery	-13.6	30.2	-43.8
Petroleum Products	9.8	44.2	-34.4
Paper Products	1.3	29.2	-27.9
Power Generation Equipment	-6.3	14.9	-21.2
Telecommunications	56.9	68.8	-11.9
Dyestuffs	12.0	9.0	-3.0
Chemicals	19.6	19.0	+0.6

Source: CSO Business Monitor 1986–1994
NOTE: errors may occur due to rounding.

generate increased export sales for UK industry as quickly as the markets in the rest of the world.

The performance of the SIM is particularly inadequate since eight of these industries were chosen by the Commission specifically because they believed them to be the potentially greatest net beneficiaries of the advent of the SIM. Whilst it is too early to draw firm conclusions concerning whether the SIM will prove harmful or beneficial to the whole of UK industry in the long run, this industry study highlights areas of clear concern. Undue concentration on the SIM's elusive export potential may mean that potentially more lucrative export markets outside the EU remain under-developed.

MAASTRICHT TREATY CONVERGENCE CRITERIA

The Maastricht Treaty was agreed between the governments of EU member states on 10 December 1991. It followed previous attempts to create EMU, starting with the Werner report in 1970, the 'Snake' in 1973–79, and the EMS established in 1979 to achieve currency stability as a preliminary to future moves towards EMU.

Article 3a of the Maastricht Treaty states that "close co-ordination of Member States' economic policies" requires:

> "...the irrevocable fixing of exchange rates leading to the introduction of a single currency ... and conduct of a single monetary policy and exchange rate policy the primary objective of both of which shall be to maintain price stability."

To achieve EMU, the Treaty envisages three stages:

- all member states are required to become members of the EMS and to remove exchange controls;

- the creation of a European Central Bank pursuing an independent EU monetary policy;

- the adoption of a single EU currency with the European Central Bank assuming full responsibility for the monetary policy of all participating nations.

No country can progress to the third stage until a majority of the European Council accepts that it fulfils four convergence criteria. These are:

- annual inflation within 1.5% of the average rate of the three EU countries where it is lowest;

- average yearly long term interest rates must be within 2% of the rates prevailing within the same countries chosen for condition (i);

- budget deficits must not be regarded 'excessive' by the Council. Article 104c (2) defines excessive government deficits as those that exceed 3% of GDP for reasons other than those of a temporary or exceptional nature, and where government debt is above 60% of GDP and is not declining at a satisfactory pace;

- two year membership of the narrow band of the ERM without a downwards alignment of the currency during this time.

Under the terms of the Maastricht Treaty, any member state meeting the convergence criteria is *legally obliged* to participate in stage three even if it believed that participation would be against its own or the wider European interest. Britain has opted-out of this provision, by requiring a separate decision to be taken by the UK government and Parliament before entry to Stage Three. However, irrespective of whether the UK eventually participates in the third stage of EMU, it is compelled to *conform* to the convergence criteria by virtue of its ratification of the Maastricht Treaty. Therefore the UK must confine its economic policy within EU norms of inflation and interest rates, must sooner or later rejoin the ERM despite the disastrous previous period of membership, and must reduce budget deficits below 3% of GDP irrespective of national priorities. Consequently, if it enters a recession or is hit by an external shock which increases inflation or unemployment, monetary and fiscal policy cannot respond to compensate for the damage done to the real economy because of an enforced preoccupation with meeting the convergence criteria.

The Maastricht fiscal convergence criteria (MFCC) constitute one reason why Kenneth Clarke has proved reluctant to introduce the tax cuts which many in his own party regard as essential for the continuance of the Conservative Party in government beyond 1997. The Chancellor wants to keep his options open about whether the UK could join EMU if it begins to operate in 1999. To comply with the Maastricht requirement of reducing the budget deficit below 3% of GDP, the March 1993 budget sought to increase taxation by £17.5 billion over three years, and in total taxes were raised by the equivalent of 7 pence on income tax or about £1,000 for every UK family. Government spending was simultaneously reduced by £15 billion in real terms as public sector growth was held at only 1% per annum over the following three years. Central government running costs were also to be squeezed between 1993–98, implying a 10% real reduction. Cutbacks on housing benefit, mortgage interest relief, education and health, in addition to a 5% real increase in fuel duty, a 3% real increase in tobacco tax, the introduction of an airport tax and the extremely unpopular VAT on domestic fuel were also part of the Maastricht process. Without the pressure to meet the convergence criteria, these substantial tax rises and public expenditure reductions could have been alternatively used to lower the basic rate of income tax below 18%.

Re-orientating economic policy to meet the MFCC prevents concentration upon meeting the national interest. Production and growth forgone as a result can be an enormous loss for a nation (see ERM section). Moreover, this amount is cumulative, so a loss in potential growth in one year is compounded by lower economic growth rates in following years from an inevitably smaller base. For example, if economic growth in the UK's GDP of approximately £600 billion is reduced from a potential 3% to only 2% by restrictive economic policy to meet the Maastricht criteria, this is equivalent to 1% or £6 billion in that year. However, since future economic growth rates now apply to a GDP of £612 billion and not £618 billion, the one-off loss is compounded in every following year. Over only one decade, assuming consistent growth rates of 3%, the cumulative effect would enlarge the initial loss to £7.98 billion, after 50 years to approximately £15.9 billion and so forth at constant prices.

In the UK's case, public sector cuts and tax increases were phased in over two to three years, and further determination to keep budget deficits below 3% in future years will impose avoidable restraints upon UK growth in the longer term. Advocates of a balanced economy across the trade cycle do not seek a balance between income and expenditure in any one year, whether in the middle of a boom or deep in recession. The 3% limit to budget deficits ignores such basic reality. It is completely arbitrary, restricting the ability of a sovereign nation to manage its own economic affairs in the interests of its own citizens. It sacrifices this priceless democratic right to an integrationist ideology which mistakes financial convergence for real convergence of economic indicators such as growth rates, national wealth per capita, industrial productivity and full employment.

The UK is not the only country to suffer from the Maastricht requirements. Germany froze social security benefits and introduced public expenditure cuts, Spain transferred responsibility for unemployment insurance to the private sector, Italy reduced public expenditure by £4.3 billion in 1993, Denmark reduced unemployment benefits, the Netherlands restricted housing benefit, Belgium introduced welfare cuts amounting to £500 million to reduce the budget deficit by 0.5% of GDP, Austria introduced budget austerity measures to reduce the budget deficit by 1.4% of GDP, and Sweden has endured 4 years of public sector cuts and tax increases, which paralysed large sections of its economy in an attempt to harmonise its economic policy with the EU mainstream. The recent French industrial unrest is a classic instance of the economic waste and the social distress generated by the Maastricht process.

To date, however, these reductions in the welfare of member states' citizens have proved insufficient to meet all the con vergence criteria, currently achieved by only Luxembourg (Table 2.4, overleaf). Even Germany cannot meet the deflationary targets, despite being the most powerful European economy. Indeed, if the same criteria were applied to the world's strongest and most dynamic economies, they would also largely fail to conform with what are essentially an arbitrarily selected range of monetary targets which have marginal importance only when measuring real economic convergence. For example, the world's two most powerful economies, the United States of America and Japan, fail to meet the Maastricht criteria since their government debt is 70% and 80% of GDP, respectively. Moreover, three of the Asian 'Tiger' economies, South Korea, Taiwan and Hong Kong, would be excluded by virtue of having excessive inflation, despite their growth rates dwarfing the paltry efforts achieved by EU member states at least partially caused by the deflationary imperative of the Maastricht convergence criteria itself.

Table 2.4

Table showing whether EU member states meet the Maastricht Convergence Criteria

Country	Inflation (%)	long-term interest rates (%)	budget deficit (%)	govt debt (%)	ERM
MFCC	3.0%	7.3%	3.0%	60.0%	yes
Austria	yes	yes	no (5.5%)	no (68%)	yes
Belgium	yes	yes	no (4.5%)	no (134%)	yes
Denmark	yes	yes	yes	no (74%)	yes
Finland	yes	yes	no (5.4%)	no (63%)	no
France	yes	yes	no (5.4%)	yes	yes
Germany	yes	yes	no (3.6%)	yes	yes
Greece	no (9.7%)	no (17.8%)	no (9.3%)	no (114%)	no
Ireland	yes	yes	yes	no (86%)	yes
Italy	no (5.2%)	no (12.3%)	no (7.4%)	no (125%)	no
Luxembourg	yes	yes	yes	yes	yes
Netherlands	yes	yes	no (3.5%)	no (78%)	yes
Portugal	no (4.3%)	no (11.6%)	no (5.4%)	no (70%)	no
Spain	no (4.8%)	no (11.4%)	no (6.0%)	no (65%)	yes
Sweden	yes	no (10.4%)	no (7.0%)	no (81%)	no
UK	yes	yes	no (4.75%)	yes	no

Source: *Sunday Times* 14/1/1996,4

Even more pain is scheduled for most EU countries if they are to participate in the third stage of EMU which offers few economic benefits in compensation. Holland (1995) documented the draconian effects of fulfilling the MFCC. If the twelve member states before the 1995 enlargement each met the 60% debt target by the end of 1999, GDP would be reduced by 2.6% each year; an unprecedented voluntary loss of wealth! The implications for employment are even more drastic. Currently there are 17.5 million people out of work in the EU, of whom more than 5 million are under the age of 25. Achieving the Maastricht criteria will worsen this grave situation. Every 10% of debt reduction in the excess countries will reduce employment by approximately 1.5 million. Meeting the 60% debt stock requirement in full would cut jobs by over 10 million, whilst even fulfilling the 3% annual deficit target would increase unemployment by around one million. The UK should take note and refuse to participate in a collective process of economic suicide.

CHAPTER III

Future Costs of the EU: Economic and Monetary Union

INTRODUCTION

The Maastricht Treaty stipulated that full economic and monetary union (EMU), together with the adoption of a single EU currency, would commence between 1997 and 1st January 1999. The speculative crises of 1992 and 1993 ensured that the earlier date cannot be met, but the strong possibility is that by 1999 at least some of the EU member states will launch a single currency. Although a Protocol agreed at Maastricht provides the UK with the opportunity to opt-out, the European Monetary Institute (EMI) and the EU finance ministers (including Britain's) are currently undertaking technical preparations for EMU. Monetary Union occurs when exchange rates are fixed irrevocably and therefore predates a single currency, but the terms are used interchangeably here. Even the Delors Report (1989) accepted that the single internal market could operate without a common EU currency, but argued that "a single currency would clearly demonstrate the irreversibility of the move to monetary union, considerably facilitate the monetary management of the Community and avoid the transactions costs of converting currencies." These claims need to be subjected to detailed analysis, because once a single currency is established, it will be almost impossible to escape from. Therefore it is essential to prove beyond reasonable doubt that the benefits exceed the costs, prior to UK entry.

THE CASE FOR A SINGLE CURRENCY

The concept of a single EU currency has been a central objective of the EU's bureaucracy for over twenty years since the Werner Report (EC Commission 1970). Some were attracted by the ability to create a counterpart to the US dollar; others advocated it for political symbolism; a further group saw it as a way of importing a model that appeared to operate effectively in Germany, the EU's major economy. These views are largely based upon subjective value judgements, but an economic case for a single currency has also been made.

1. Transaction costs of multiple currencies:

Its most obvious advantage is the elimination of the transaction costs of changing EU currencies, both for the travelling public and for trading purposes. Although the costs of changing money can be considerable for individuals, they are less onerous to firms because of the higher volume of their transactions; indeed, many large companies hold balances in a range of currencies and hence rely upon internal financing. The Governor of the Bank of England claimed, in a speech to the Association of French Bankers on 31st January 1995, that even costs to the individual were overstated:

> "*Anyone who travels throughout the EU exchanging all his currency as he goes deserves to pay for the privilege – particularly in the age of the plastic card.*"

The Commission estimated that transactions costs can amount to at least 0.4% of the EU's GDP each year (EC Commission 1990). However, this gain will not be distributed equally across member states. Savings for the UK will be below average for two reasons:

The UK's intra-EU trade is less significant than for most EU countries, therefore a higher proportion of UK trade will still require currency exchange. The relative importance of intra-EU visible imports and exports is much less for the UK than for the Benelux countries, for example (Table 3.1). Less than half of Britain's total trade is with other EU members and only

Table 3.1

Intra-EU visible trade (1988)

Country	% of GDP
Belgium & Luxembourg	87.3
Ireland	77.3
Netherlands	63.1
Portugal	44.8
Greece	27.3
Denmark	25.9
Germany	25.6
France	23.8
UK	20.9
Italy	18.3
Spain	17.1

Source: EC Commission 1990

approximately 30% is with those countries most likely to proceed with EMU in 1999.

Domestic foreign exchange services are relatively efficient in the UK, so that transactions costs are lower than in many EU member states.

The savings to the UK from reduced transactions costs could therefore be half the EU average, implying a saving of around 0.2% of UK GDP per annum, which is equivalent to £1.2 billion. The figure will be even lower if certain countries either voluntarily opt-out of the EMU process or cannot meet the Maastricht convergence criteria. Moreover, it must be offset against the loss in revenue suffered by the banking sector.

2. Lower exchange rate variability:

A second benefit claimed for the adoption of a single currency is a reduction in exchange rate variability. It is argued that volatile exchange rates exert a damaging effect upon investment and growth. The EC Commission (1990, 63) estimated that;

> "... even a reduction in the risk premium of only 0.5% points could raise income in the Community significantly, possibly by up to 5–10% in the long run."

Such grandiose claims are not supported by academic research, the weight of which concludes that there is no relationship between exchange rate volatility and trade (De Grauwe 1992). Even the EC Commission (1990, 73) acknowledges this, stating that:

> "Since the empirical research has not found any robust relationship between exchange rate variability and trade, it is not possible to estimate the increase in intra-EU trade that might derive from the irrevocable fixing of exchange rates."

Recent EU-specific studies confirm the finding. Frankel and Wei (1993) estimated that the doubling of exchange rate variability inside the EMS after the summer of 1992 resulted in a fall in trade volumes amongst EMS countries of just 0.25%. Sapir, Sekkhat and Weber (1994) could discover "no apparent link between trade volumes and exchange rate variability in bilateral intra- and extra-Community trade and exchange rate data."

Even if it is accepted that exchange rate fluctuations generate a mis-allocation of resources, the price of eliminating them may be greater. The costs of suppressing exchange rate volatility are often large, including unemployment, low growth, subsidies and protectionism. It is frequently assumed that eliminating exchange rate risk reduces the real rate of interest and hence generates higher growth, but due to lower demand it also reduces firms' expected future profits, so that the net effect is ambiguous.

3. Lower inflation rates:

The EC Commission (1990, 87) argued that many of the gains from EMU derive from the supposed benefits of the lower inflation it is expected to induce. Where an economy functions through the price mechanism, any disruption to it generates sub-optimal outcomes. Inflation causes time and effort to be expended coping with expected future price levels; pensioners see their savings reduced and workers their real wages, and throughout the economy people are subjected to 'menu costs' as prices are regularly increased. Prioritising low inflation above other economic policy objectives, the Commission asserts that the institutions to be introduced under EMU, based on the German model of central bank control, would eliminate inflation to the extent that it ceases to affect peoples' decision-making. The main promoter of price stability will be the operation of monetary policy by an independent European Central Bank (ECB) with its institutional "primary objective ... to maintain price stability" (Article 105, Cmnd. 1934); it might stimulate investment since firms can better judge their future prospects in a low inflation environment. When inflation expectations are lower, governments can use budgetary policy to run the economy at higher levels of output and employment. The EC Commission (1990, 87) estimated that the direct benefit to the EU of lower inflation would be of the order of 0.3% of EU GDP, which is additional to the gains already referred to in respect of higher income growth.

Clearly the Commission's analysis is designed to portray EMU favourably, but it is untested. Price stability is not guaranteed under a single currency for at least three reasons:

- under the Maastricht Treaty, decisions in exchange rate policy remain outside the remit of the ECB, being taken by the European Council. Consequently conflicts between exchange rate policy and the pursuit of price stability could potentially occur and their resolution is problematic. The wording of the relevant statutes, that exchange rate decisions will be taken only after consultation with the ECB, is ambiguous;

- the federal structure of the ECB may result in a higher

tolerance for inflation than currently exists in Germany, the dominant ERM country that determines the monetary stance of other participants. If the decisions of the ECB reflect an average attitude to inflation, 'price stability' may be interpreted on a looser definition. Dissatisfaction with German economic policy dominance is one source of pressure for an ECB, where Germany is just one, albeit important, of a number of voices;

- even if the ECB can devote itself to achieving EU price stability, it may be unable to attain its target because of the technical difficulties of operating an EU-wide monetary policy. The European Monetary Institute is due to report on these problems before the end of 1996; they should not be underestimated. They include how price stability is to be measured, selection of the indicator(s) at which policy is targeted and the choice of the tools through which policy is implemented. All these decisions incur problematic consequences, particularly because the short-run relationship between the money supply and economic activity varies between EU member states.

As a new institution, the ECB will inevitably need time to establish credibility. Unless and until this is achieved, an inflation-risk premium is likely to apply to EU interest rates. Nor is EMU a necessary prerequisite for eliminating such a premium. It can be achieved, without the need of costly, unpredictable negotiations, by the consistent application of domestic economic policy. The experience of Switzerland demonstrates how a reputation for minimal inflation, obtained domestically, yields low interest rates. It has been claimed that globalisation has removed national control of economic policy. The evidence, however, suggests otherwise. UK policy must take account of developments elsewhere, but is not determined by them. For instance, sterling's weakness against the deutschmark in February and March 1995 would, under fixed exchange rates, have required a rise in British interest rates to maintain sterling's external value. The UK authorities chose not to pursue such a strategy. Thus the UK enjoys a degree of independence, whose inevitable loss is a cost of joining EMU. Its nature and extent is discussed subsequently.

4. Deterrence of destabilising currency speculation:

A further argument for a single currency is that it will deter speculators from 'picking off' individual currencies, as in the ERM crises of 1992 and 1993, by replacing them with one EU-wide money backed by the combined resources of participating central banks. In an international economy where some £190 billion is currently traded daily in the London Forex market, 90% of which are speculative funds unrelated to trade (Jones 1995), such an argument has appeal. However, it ignores the fact that most speculation originates outside the EU, that a single currency could be the focus of speculation against the dollar or the yen, that other measures such as a transactions tax can curb speculation (Tobin 1994) and that a single currency imposes heavy and certain costs upon the UK. It is to these that we now turn.

THE CASE AGAINST A SINGLE CURRENCY

The actual process by which a single currency is achieved will involve transition costs. EMU effectively occurs when the Maastricht Treaty's Stage Three commences, which is likely to be 1st January 1999. On this date, participating countries will irrevocably lock their exchange rates at fixed, yet to be determined, rates of convertibility. These countries by definition form a monetary union, since each is unable to follow an independent monetary policy. However, until national currencies cease to exist, the ECB must ensure that the locked exchange rates are maintained. Whilst it can draw upon the pooled reserves of national central banks, the transitional period involves risks, especially if EMU economies diverge and financial markets put pressure on the parities. Moreover, crucial issues, such as when the single currency will be introduced and for how long (or even if) it co-exists alongside national currencies, remain unresolved. Whatever the decisions taken, transaction costs will be incurred.

Adjustment costs of a single currency:

)ving to a single currency provides a major upheaval for all economic agents. For consumers, the costs are mainly in adjusting to a new monetary value system. The costs on business involve the changeover in record and accounting systems coupled to a temporary need to express prices in terms of both the national and the single EU currency. Such costs will fall disproportionately upon small firms. The only area where the burden of transition has been estimated is the banking sector. The European Banking Federation calculated that EU banks need to spend between £6.3 and £7.9 billion to implement a single currency over three to four years (Taylor 1995, 20). This amounts to 2% of operating costs for each changeover year, a sum over £900 million per annum for the UK banking sector. If the assumption of a three to four year adjustment proves an under-estimate, the costs would be materially greater. The cost for the government would certainly not be negligible either, since the UK would have to give away almost 80% of its total official reserves to the proposed European Central Bank (ECB) to be established in Germany. This would represent a sum of £22.93 billion, or equivalent to £395 for every man, woman and child in the UK, and it could not be recovered if the UK subsequently decided to pull out of the single currency. This is in addition to the estimated £70 million the UK has already paid to the European Monetary Institute to assist it in establishing the ECB and devising the single currency – a currency which it would not be in Britain's best interests to join.

The transition to a single currency might also affect the demand for money. The relationship between monetary indicators and demand could become less stable, not only across the EU, but within individual countries, because the total demand for a single currency is unlikely to be simply the sum of the demand for money in member states. Consequently, large, unpredictable shifts in the demand for money will generate either a Community-wide inflationary or deflationary shock, which add significantly to transition costs. The former will damage the ECB's credibility, whilst the latter could threaten the entire EMU project.

2. Intra-union trade differences:

After such adjustment burdens have been borne, EMU becomes still more costly. There are no general principles implying that a single currency is intrinsically beneficial; if it was, a global currency would top the policy agenda. Therefore each proposal must be assessed on the basis of its specific advantages and disadvantages. Usually currency union projects are beneficial where participants exhibit similarities of intra-union trade and economic structure; if they display great differences, unions are detrimental. In the case of the UK within the EU, the differences are substantial, so that a single currency involves greater costs than benefits.

Analysis of trade with other EU member states demonstrates that less than half of all UK trade (around 47%) occurs within the EU (Taylor 1995, 28; Table 3.2). A breakdown highlights a substantial contrast between the relative importance of visible and invisible trade with the rest of the EU. In terms of goods, over half of both exports and imports are with other EU members (in 1993, 57% and 55% respectively). The structure of invisible trade, almost as important to the UK for exports, is radically different. In 1993, the EU accounted for only 36.3% of invisible exports from, and 36.7% of invisible imports to, the UK. Since the UK is relatively more efficient at producing services, which are the most rapidly expanding area of international trade, these proportions are highly significant.

Subdivision of EU countries into a 'core' containing Germany, France, the Netherlands, Austria, Belgium and Luxembourg (those most likely to initiate moves towards a single currency) and the rest is revealing. The core accounts for only 30% of total UK trade (visible plus invisible) so even if Britain entered EMU with them, in 1999, around 70% of its trade by value will remain subject to a currency exchange. Distinguishing between visible and invisible trade, only 22.8% of UK invisible exports and 25.6% of invisible imports are with core countries, and as a result, benefits to the UK from transaction cost savings will be relatively small.

Table 3.2

UK Visible and Invisible Trade, 1993 (£bn)

Countries	Exports			Imports		
	Visible	Invisible	Total	Visible	Invisible	Total
'Core' EU						
Germany	16.0	10.0	26.0	19.9	10.0	29.9
France	12.1	6.0	18.1	13.4	8.3	21.7
Netherlands	8.1	5.5	13.6	9.0	5.3	14.3
Austria	0.9	0.9	1.8	0.9	0.9	1.8
Belgium/Lux	7.1	3.9	11.0	6.7	4.6	11.3
TOTAL	44.2	26.3	70.5	49.9	29.1	79.0
Other EU						
Denmark	1.6	1.2	2.8	2.1	1.0	3.1
Finland	1.1	0.9	2.0	1.8	0.4	2.2
Greece	0.9	0.6	1.5	0.3	1.2	1.5
Ireland	6.3	2.4	8.7	5.4	2.1	7.5
Italy	6.1	6.2	12.3	6.6	2.5	9.1
Portugal	1.4	0.5	1.9	1.2	0.9	2.1
Spain	4.4	1.8	6.2	3.2	3.5	6.7
Sweden	2.9	2.0	4.9	3.5	0.9	4.4
TOTAL	24.7	15.6	40.3	24.1	12.5	36.6
TOTAL–EU	68.7	41.9	110.8	74.0	41.6	115.6
NON–EU	52.5	73.6	126.1	60.6	71.9	132.5
WORLD TOTAL	121.4	115.5	236.9	134.6	113.5	248.1
'Core' EU as % of World Total	36.4	22.8	29.8	37.1	25.6	31.8
Total EU as % of World Total	56.8	36.3	46.8	55.0	36.7	46.6

Source: Economic Trends, March 1995

Table 3.3

UK Overseas Direct Investment, 1993 (£bn)

Countries	UK Overseas Investment		Overseas Investment in UK	
	flow in year	year end stock	flow in year	year end stock
'Core' EU				
Germany	1.4	5.9	0.7	5.9
France	0.6	8.4	–	8.0
Netherlands	3.0	23.6	1.2	18.2
Austria	–	0.4	–	–
Belgium/Lux	0.2	2.7	- 0.4	1.8
TOTAL	5.2	41.0	1.5	33.9
Other EU				
Denmark	0.2	1.3	–	1.8
Finland	–	0.1	–	0.3
Greece	0.1	0.3	–	–
Ireland	0.8	4.2	0.1	0.7
Italy	0.3	2.3	0.1	0.9
Portugal	–	1.2	–	–
Spain	–	2.9	–	0.3
Sweden	0.1	0.9	–	2.5
TOTAL	1.5	13.2	0.2	6.5
TOTAL-EU	6.7	54.2	1.7	40.4
NON-EU	10.3	111.0	7.5	79.5
WORLD TOTAL	17.0	165.2	9.2	119.9
'Core' EU as % of World Total	30.6	24.8	16.3	28.3
Total EU as % of World Total	39.4	32.8	18.5	33.7

Source: CSO

In the context of EMU, UK investment patterns reinforce those of trade; most overseas investment by UK companies is not located in the EU and most overseas investment in the UK does not come from the EU (Table 3.3). In 1993, around 30% of overseas investment was in the EU core and around 25% of the total stock of UK overseas investment was located there. Only 16.3% of investment originated from the core countries but 28.3% of the stock of overseas investment came from them. Thus, at least 70% of overseas investment by, or to, UK companies would remain subject to exchange rate uncertainty if the UK decided to proceed to a single currency.

Extending the analysis to all other EU countries does not increase these proportions to near 50%. At the end of 1993 only one-third of the stock of overseas investment was located in EU member states, even though almost 40% of that year's overseas investment went to EU nations. Similarly, whilst 33.7% of the stock of overseas investment in the UK originated within the EU, only 18.5% of investment flowing into the UK in 1993 came from EU member states.

Such differences indicate that the British economy does not move in step with other EU countries, from which it varies in structure. These are not the conditions under which it is wise for the UK to relinquish its independent monetary policy, particularly the ability to adjust its exchange rate. Moreover, any enlargement to the east would render the EU even more economically heterogeneous and still further away from an optimum currency area. Nor have any reasons been provided as to why structural differences between EU members will disappear after EMU. These arguments in reverse suggest that the case for monetary union is strongest for Germany and the Benelux countries; indeed, they already operate as though they used a single currency. Other countries would be unwise to join them.

3. Differences in intra-union economies:

EMU also imposes substantial costs upon member states which face asymmetrical shocks. If shocks impact differentially across countries, either because their initial impact varies or because national economic structures diverge, the ability to adjust by changing the nominal exchange rate can alleviate the harmful consequences of such shocks. EMU, however, is less efficient at absorbing asymmetric disturbances across countries than a regime involving separate currencies. A detailed study by Bayoumi and Eichengreen (1992) isolated the aggregate demand and supply shocks that impact on national economies within the EU. They showed that between 1960 and 1988 the correlation of both demand and supply shocks that affected the UK with those affecting Germany was low. They also demonstrated that, in addition to the weak correlation, the size of those shocks is relatively large. Clearly, for the UK, the EU does not resemble the 'optimum currency area' envisaged by economists.

These findings are reinforced because Britain's economic structure varies fundamentally from those of other EU countries, in ways that would differentiate its response to an EU-wide economic policy from that required for successful currency areas:

- Oil production – the UK and the Netherlands are the only significant oil and gas producers in the EU. Any change to oil or gas prices therefore exerts a different effect in those countries than on other EU members and thus requires an alternative policy stance;

- Manufacturing and services – there is a noticeable difference between the relative significance of these sectors within the UK and Germany. Manufacturing is more important in Germany than in the UK (30% compared to 23% of GDP), but the proportionate role of financial and media services is greater in the UK than in Germany or the rest of the EU;

- External trade – the UK, Italy, and Spain rely least on other EU members for external trade (Table 3.1). Not only does this mean that potential transaction cost savings are lower in these countries, but also that movements in the ECU exchange rate with external currencies impact more heavily on them. A depreciation of the ECU against the dollar or yen, for instance, amounts to a greater relaxation of monetary policy in the UK than in the Netherlands;

Table 3.4

Interest Payments as a Proportion of Income (%), 1990

Country	Household Sector	Corporate Sector
Belgium	2.4	44
France	3.7	33
Germany	3.2	26
Ireland	2.2	n/a
Italy	4.0	31
Netherlands	3.6	30
Spain	4.2	24
Portugal	2.6	52
UK	10.9	24

Source: Miles, D., Bank of England Quarterly Bulletin, February 1994

- Corporate and household debt – the UK carries a much higher proportion of debt paid at variable rates of interest, in both the corporate and household sectors, than the rest of the EU. Household debt comprises a larger proportion of GDP than in other EU member states, reflecting the different nature of the housing market (Table 3.4). The corporate sector is more reliant upon equity financing and variable interest loans in the UK than most EU nations, who tend to prefer long-term fixed-rate loan-financing for industry. As a result, the immediate deflationary impact of a given rise in interest rates is greater than in France or Germany. Therefore, even if inflationary pressures were identical throughout the currency area before a change in monetary policy, they could not remain the same afterwards. Policy shocks in the UK will thus increase because of EMU. It is theoretically possible that a single currency may gradually reduce national differences in corporate and household balance sheets, but they are likely to persist for decades after such a currency is introduced.

Moreover, a single currency and a single market may increase national structural differences, raising the possibility of country-specific shocks. The rationale of an EU internal market is to encourage greater specialisation of production within its constituent areas. However, because regional specialisation creates more dependency on a narrow range of commodities any disturbance to a particular demand would be focused upon a specific EU locality. The substantial structural differences that already exist between the UK and the rest of the EU mean that the UK faces nationally specific shocks, both in number and size. The costs to the UK of joining a single currency, in terms of the output and employment lost from abandoning an independent economic policy, are significant. Ominously they will increase rather than diminish over time, because the UK is both insufficiently integrated with, and sufficiently different from, the countries most likely to participate in a single currency.

4. Loss of economic sovereignty:

The removal of the nominal exchange rate as a means of adjustment goes beyond the crucial role of mitigating the effects of the trade cycle. The real exchange rate, which is the nominal exchange rate adjusted for the price level, changes over time to reflect the impact of shocks, both permanent and temporary, and of trends in such influences as productivity growth and consumer tastes which inevitably vary between countries. Thus, lower productivity growth in the UK compared to its trading partners needs to be reflected in a lower real exchange rate, which can be achieved either by a lower nominal exchange rate or a reduced domestic price level. Because price levels rarely adjust speedily, the nominal exchange rate is particularly effective in achieving real exchange movements.

Currently, the UK enjoys considerable economic sovereignty, reflected by its scope to increase demand to emerge from the early 1990s recession accentuated by its ERM membership. Such scope was increased by departure from the ERM in September 1992. However, any movement towards EMU would reverse the process towards greater economic self-governance. If the EU were to possess a single currency, a single ECB is required to issue it. Although Britain would be represented on the ECB board and would exercise some influence over its decisions, it would effectively and permanently lose control of its monetary policy. Decisions about targets for money supply growth, and the interest rates needed to achieve them, would presumably be taken by some kind of weighted majority voting. Given the disparities of economic structure between member states, these decisions would often not be suited to UK circumstances.

5. Central bank independence:

The Maastricht Treaty (Article 107) stipulates that the ECB will be independent of governments and that its sole legislative task is to achieve price stability. Despite the acknowledged success of the German Bundesbank, at least until the 1990 unification, there is no evidence that in general independent central banks generate lower rates of inflation (Baimbridge & Burkitt 1995d & e), whilst ECB independence removes economic decision-making from democratically elected politicians to non-accountable bankers (Burkitt & Baimbridge 1994b). Moreover, if low inflation is regarded as only one objective of economic policy and it is believed that all the instruments available to governments should be deployed to achieve other targets (including full employment, growth and a sustainable balance of payments), the prospect of an undemocratic ECB geared entirely to the pursuit of price stability is destructive of economic welfare. Therefore an independent ECB should be opposed because it precludes democratic control of monetary policy. Nor are its claimed benefits real. There is no evidence that low or zero inflation generates a higher rate of economic growth or that independent central banks guarantee low inflation and nor that the costs of inflation are high compared to those of unemployment (Baimbridge & Burkitt 1995d & e).

An independent ECB creates a situation where one group (elected representatives) is in charge of fiscal policy and another group (unelected central bankers) controls monetary policy. Such a separation of responsibilities rests on the fallacy that these policies are independent. They are not. If the government's stance is to run a budget deficit (both a common case an necessary in many circumstances), its size and method of finance carry monetary implications (Baimbridge & Burkitt 1995c). Whether it is financed by borrowing from the bank or non-bank sectors possesses different consequences for monetary measures. It is inefficient to determine fiscal and monetary policy independently, which is one reason why the Bank of England was nationalised in 1945. Certainly, if the ECB fixes monetary policy, the fiscal choices remaining for a government within EMU are circumscribed.

6. The failure of fiscal federalism:

The introduction of a single currency would prevent any member state from devaluing or revaluing. Thus, if any country became less competitive, as is frequently inevitable in a dynamic world, it could not restore balance of payments equilibrium by altering its exchange rate. Devaluation does not provide a permanent cure for loss of competitiveness because it is unlikely to alter the factors which cause it, but it is an immediate way of restoring competitiveness at a particular time. If exchange rate flexibility is removed, a lack of competitiveness becomes difficult to remedy (Burkitt & Baimbridge 1994a).

Such a problem, however, no longer leads to a balance of payments deficit within a single currency area. Instead it takes a different form. Unless relative costs can be reduced or productivity increased, output and employment will fall. Without large-scale emigration, joblessness will rise, and high unemployment and a depressed level of income may become chronic. An analogy can be drawn between the position in which Britain might find itself under a single EU currency and that of Scotland and Wales within the UK. Throughout most of the twentieth century Scotland and Wales experienced greater unemployment and lower levels of per capita income than the South of England, but their competitive disadvantages cannot be overcome by devaluation because they share a common currency with England.

The same difficulties would confront member states if the EU adopted a single currency. Britain, located on the geographical periphery of the EU, and with a history of money wages rising faster and productivity more slowly than in some of its neighbours, could be particularly at risk. Moreover, these dangers are greater within the EU than in the UK. Individual countries possess powerful equilibrating mechanisms that moderate regional disparities, but they would not exist in a single currency EU.

One of these mechanisms is the mobility of labour. A common culture and a common language make migration from high to low unemployment regions in Britain a relatively easy procedure. Moving from the UK to other EU members in search of work is a more formidable undertaking. The Commission found that migration between member countries in the first half of the 1980s was just 25% of migration across USA states in the same period. Moreover, the stock of migrants living in EU member states, the presence of whom may attract additional foreign workers, is relatively small. In Denmark, Finland, Greece, Italy, Portugal and Spain, for instance, the number of foreign residents from within the EU make up less than 1% of the total working population; in France, Germany, Ireland, Netherlands, Sweden and the UK this figure is less than 3%; and it is only in Belgium and Luxembourg where this is exceeded (Frankland 1996). Furthermore, in all countries except Belgium and Luxembourg, which are in many respects special cases, non-EU nationals comfortably exceed migrants from EU nations, thereby signifying that most member states are more internationally orientated than advocates of further integration realise. Nor will a single currency increase labour mobility since it does not affect the main inhibiting factors. Consequently labour mobility is unlikely to contribute to an equalisation of unemployment across an EU-wide single currency area.

A more important equilibrator is government. In a unitary state like Britain, and to a lesser but still significant extent in a federal nation like the USA, the activities of central government exert a major impact on the regional pattern of output, incomes and employment. In Britain, social security benefits and tax rates are identical in all parts of the country. Resources are therefore channelled automatically from prosperous to depressed areas. Because, for instance, education and health care provision is notionally the same throughout Britain, teachers and NHS workers possess jobs and spend money even in low-income, high unemployment regions. They also provide income in kind, in the form of free or subsidised services distributed fairly equally across the nation. Grants from central to local government, which help to finance a variety of other public services, also reduce geographical disparities. Additionally, throughout most of the post-war period, specific regional subsidies and incentives have been provided by governments to stimulate the growth of more depressed regions.

German reunification was facilitated by the state. The decision to replace the Ostmark one-for-one with the Deutschmark endowed East Germany with an enormously over-valued currency, which caused a loss of competitiveness and unemployment. The East German economy was only protected from the full consequences by political and budgetary unification generating an enormous transfer of wealth from the West. Even so, the social costs of reunification, especially in terms of unemployment and its many consequences such as outbreaks of racial violence, will probably persist.

These government equilibrating activities are possible only because of the size of central government budgets (typically 40 to 45% of GDP in unitary advanced industrial states and 20 to 25% in federations, which often possess explicit fiscal equalisation schemes). By contrast, the EU budget is currently 1.2% of its GDP. Over half is spent on the CAP, whose impact on regional inequalities tends to be regressive; for instance, in the mid-1980s, Denmark had the highest per capita income of the ten members yet received the second highest per capita subsidies from the CAP. Less than a fifth of the budget is specifically designed to assist EU regions with relatively low income or high unemployment.

The budget size of 1.2% of GDP is derisory compared to the figure of 7.5 to 10% which an expert group, set up by the EC Commission under Sir Donald MacDougall in 1977, concluded was the minimum required if EMU was not to generate un-acceptable disparities in living standards (MacDougall 1977 & 1992). The subsequent accession of Greece, Portugal and Spain raised that minimum, as did the growth of unemployment after 1977 and the increase in its dispersion around the average. For instance, in December 1994, unemployment in the EU varied from 3.5% in Luxembourg, 4% in Austria and 6% in Germany, to 15% in Ireland, 18.5% in Finland and 24% in Spain (EU Commission 1995). The imposition of a single currency given such real economic divergence would generate intolerable economic and political friction's within the EU. Nor could a high unemployment member expect support from its EMU colleagues. Article 104(b) of the Maastricht Treaty specifically rules out a financial rescue of one country by another.

The 1992 Edinburgh summit agreed an EU budget increase to no more than 1.3% of GDP by the year 2000. It is hard to envisage the existence of the political will to raise this figure in the foreseeable future. Consequently a single currency will exacerbate regional inequalities and generate greater unemployment. Britain could become a low-income, slow-growth, high-unemployment area of the EU. Indeed, increased unemployment is the only way a national economy could adjust to a fall in competitiveness, given an absence of the large growth in labour mobility and/or in the EU budget, which are both potential equilibrating mechanisms.

While the Maastricht Treaty does not propose creating a supranational fiscal authority, such a body would be required should EMU take place. Once established, its role and objectives will expand. The need to mitigate the effects of shocks will extend into permanent transfers of resources in an attempt to achieve 'social cohesion', but without the political acceptance that sustains similar transfers within a nation. The need for central public finances under EMU, combined with the drive by the Commission and certain member states towards European political union, will inevitably result in fiscal union or EU collapse. The former is detrimental to the UK and the uncertainty increased by a sudden EU collapse would undermine the short term prospects of all nations who remained members.

The need to achieve permanent resource transfers to mitigate the impact of a single currency will add significantly to the overall tax burden. Since the EU is already taxed more heavily than its international competitors, especially the USA and Japan, the additional tax imposition would damage EU competitiveness. The consequent rise in unemployment would put further strain on public finances, creating a vicious circle of heavier taxes leading to reduced competitiveness, generating greater unemployment and further tax increases. The EU is a sub-optimal currency area, because under EMU the combination of asymmetrical shocks and the lack of effective adjustment mechanisms will result in greater regional income disparities.

The EC Commission (1990, 168) implicitly acknowledges the negative impact of EMU on regional inequalities. It states that:

> "... *collective welfare considerations in EMU could lead to the decision to reduce [the impact] by enhancing the role of public finance.*"

If such transfers do not take place, some countries will possess an incentive to withdraw from EMU, so damaging its credibility. The EC Commission (1990, 168) concluded that:

> "... *enhanced central public finance may therefore serve as an insurance for the credibility of the system.*"

The Maastricht Treaty federalist package is almost impossible to unravel given the difficulties of its ratification, but it is a recipe for still greater unemployment and poverty. EU unemployment is presently at record levels. According to official estimates almost twenty million people lack work. However, the economic provisions of the Maastricht Treaty do not address the problem of how to restore full employment, but instead imposed a series of deflationary proposals. Holland (1995) summarised the conclusions of recent research estimating the impact of meeting the Maastricht fiscal convergence criteria between 1994 and the end of 1999. For the twelve members before enlargement, it means reducing GDP by 2.6% each year. Such voluntary renunciations of wealth are unprecedented. Achieving the 3% annual PSBR targets would cut employment by nearly a million, whilst attaining the 60% national debt stock objectives would reduce jobs by 10 million. It is difficult to conceive of a more disastrous transition towards a single EU currency.

Consequently, a single currency would be so damaging to the peoples of Britain and Europe that it must be opposed. Not only its economic, but its political implications are grave. Higher unemployment breeds nationalism and racism, as the electoral fortunes of 'extreme right' parties in European Parliament elections demonstrate (Burkitt, Baimbridge & Macey 1994 and 1995). However, many economists claim that Britain will suffer if it opts out of a single currency, should some or all other EU members go ahead, whilst accepting that the project should ideally be abandoned. We now analyse that claim.

Can the UK viably opt-out of a Single Currency, if the rest of the EU goes ahead?

The weight of evidence indicates that the EU fails to satisfy the criteria for an optimal currency area for all its members. Our analysis demonstrates that a UK refusal to participate in a single currency will yield substantial benefits. If, however, other EU members go ahead, what dangers would the UK face outside? The oft-quoted problems are:

1. It is argued that countries not participating in the single currency will experience higher interest rates, because foreign exchange markets exact a 'risk premium' against currency depreciation and greater inflation. The argument may in certain situations possess some substance, but its practical validity for the UK is dubious, since it depends upon the totally unknown conduct of future economic policy in both opt-out and opt-in countries. Moreover, the impact of interest rate differentials upon long-term growth and job creation is questionable. Equally, the widespread belief that currency depreciation leads to inflation is unduly pessimistic in light of the substantial countervailing evidence (Burkitt, Baimbridge & Mills 1993).

2. Many fear that a UK opt-out might reduce inward investment, because it could become more attractive to invest in the
EMU countries. The argument cannot be sustained, given the
lack of significant transaction cost savings or benefits from
eliminating exchange rate variability. Indeed the evidence refutes
the claim; being outside the ERM in the 1980s did not curb
inward investment, rather the reverse occurred! The UK is the
largest EU recipient of inward investment, for example in 1992
Britain received £7.6 billion of direct investment from non-EU
countries (43.6% of all inward investment into the EU), despite
not being a member of the ERM. Therefore, factors other than
exchange rate stability determine the direction of capital flows.

Various influences account for British success in attracting
inward investment, but none are threatened if the UK opts out of
EMU. They include a plentiful supply of skilled labour, low non-
wage labour costs, access to all European markets, an international outlook and use of the English language. Indeed, there
are strong reasons for believing that, contrary to conventional
wisdom, inward investment to the UK would be threatened by
participation in EMU. First, the consequent likely increase in
economic instability will reduce the attractiveness of the UK as a
destination for investment. Second, UK involvement in EMU
would involve high non-wage labour costs, prevalent in the EU,
being imposed upon British business. The UK's ability to attract
investment relative to the rest of the EU would be impaired, whilst
the EU as a whole would suffer in competition for world capital
compared to countries in Asia and Latin America. A single
currency is therefore contra-indicated.

3. The City of London is one of three world financial centres
(along with New York and Tokyo), earning a surplus for the UK
balance of payments amounting to £11 billion in 1993. The City
Research Project estimates that international wholesale financial
services in Britain employ about 150,000 people and generate
between £10 and £15 billion per annum (Taylor 1992, 22). It is
often asserted that, if the UK did not participate in EMU, long-
term damage would be inflicted upon the City, which would

ultimately lose its pre-eminence to Frankfurt or even Paris, because trading in the single currency will be focused within its area of operation.

A trend exists whereby international business in any given time zone gravitates towards a single location. Centralisation is propelled by a preference for deep and liquid markets; accommodating legal, tax and regulatory frameworks; skilled labour; and a cluster of supporting services in accountancy, law, software and telecommunications. The City possesses all these and it would be very difficult for any EU competitor to emulate them.

When analysing the consequences of EMU for the City, it is crucial to distinguish between its role as the premier EU financial centre and its position as one of three world financial centres. The immediate effect of EMU is a loss of intra-EU exchange rate transactions. However, it is likely to be more than compensated by an increase in Euro-ECU transactions that will probably be concentrated in London more than, for instance, French franc-dollar business is currently. In theory, a greater threat to the City arises from the creation of an EU government bond market that is an inevitable consequence of EMU and which many hope will lead to the Euro-ECU rivalling the dollar and the yen as a world currency. The relevant EU authority will certainly attempt to domicile the new EU government debt market within its borders. However, without effective exchange controls, it would prove impossible to prevent the Euro-ECU bond market from becoming global, so that a Euro-ECU market would soon develop in London. Therefore, so long as London maintains its competitive advantage, its European pre-eminence will continue whether or not the UK participates in EMU.

However, if the UK were to join EMU, the City's position as an international financial centre will be threatened. This role is more important than its European one; for instance, two-thirds of the 350 non-UK banks represented in London are based outside the EU. It is the City's role in global markets where business is growing fastest in the economies of the Pacific Rim and South America, established to some degree by a favourable regulatory and taxation regime, that is in jeopardy if the UK enters EMU. It would be undermined further if EMU led to fiscal and political union. An EU-wide regime would be suspected of pursuing a more interventionist approach to financial services, their regulation and taxation. If a perception developed that London would become subject to a more restrictive administration (and no other EU member enjoys experience of its special position) its role as a global financial centre could diminish rapidly, to the benefit of New York or financial centres in Asia.

Consequently, it is clear that, even if some EU members sign up for the single currency, the UK should not do so. It will find that opting for economic self-governance, rapid growth and full employment means opting out of a single currency. Moreover, there need be no serious consequences if the UK does not participate in EMU. The benefits of full employment and low inflation can be achieved by pursuing coherent domestic economic policies, whilst arguments that both the role of the City of London and the UK's success in attracting inward investment would be threatened if the UK stayed out of EMU collapse under close scrutiny. Indeed, each would benefit from the UK opting-out. The UK would not be left behind if other countries proceed towards a single currency. By following independent domestic economic policies, the UK can achieve low rates of inflation with employment and competitiveness levels that will be the envy of those in the single currency area.

SUMMARY

Our analysis demonstrates that a core group of EU countries are sufficiently alike in their exposure and response to economic shocks that EMU deserves their serious consideration, whatever the ultimate decision. The UK is not, however, one of these nations. If it were to join a single currency, it would face large shocks, specific to itself, without an independent monetary (nor increasingly, budgetary) policy nor sufficiently flexible commodity and labour markets to achieve adjustment. In the absence of any other equilibrating mechanism, heavy costs would be imposed on the British economy in terms of lost output and employment. The benefits of reduced transactions costs are far outweighed by the detrimental impact on the wider economy and business in general. The UK economy is insufficiently integrated with, and sufficiently structurally different from, the countries most likely to launch a single currency. Therefore the benefits of a single currency will be lower or less likely to be achieved, and the costs higher, than if the UK economy was similar to other members. The UK suffered heavy losses of jobs and production as a consequence of following an inappropriate monetary policy during its membership of the ERM. All the evidence indicates that a single currency would generate similar consequences, except that under a single currency, having lost an independent pound sterling, there would be no escape. The conclusion is unequivocal; the UK should not join a single currency as its economic interests would be prejudiced by EMU participation.

CHAPTER IV

It'll Never Happen?

The EU integrationist project contains fundamental internal contradictions, which have led many UK politicians to assume that, whatever the rhetoric, further moves towards political and economic union are incapable of realisation. Those who share this view point to the recent retirement of Jacques Delors from Commission President, as signalling a slowdown in EU integrationist initiatives. Moreover, they argue that Chancellor Kohl is the last leader of a generation which remembers the Second World War and is therefore motivated (at least partly) by the desire to create a common European superstructure which would make another European war impossible. Without leaders of such commitment to the goal of a federal Europe, so the argument goes, the whole project will simply fall apart. A second strand to this viewpoint examines recent trends within the EU countries which suggests that further integration is not welcomed by the citizens of the EU that its member governments and the EU bureaucracy are supposed to represent. However, UK politicians since 1945 have consistently under-estimated the momentum behind EU integration; it would be disastrous for our national interests to repeat the mistake.

The EU's cross-national opinion polls (Eurobarometer 1993) demonstrate increased scepticism about further integration within most member states. The proportion of EU voters who expressed positive support for EU membership and hope for future developments has declined considerably between 1988 and 1994. Moreover, comparing opinions in twelve EU countries in 1994 with previous decades, there was a noticeable increase in the numbers who believed their country did not benefit from EU membership in seven nations, increased opposition towards a possible future EU government and towards EU membership itself in eight nations, and increased expressions of fear for the future in ten nations.

To test whether these opinions reflect a general desire to relinquish national democratic powers to European institutions, or whether it reflects the particular phraseology of the question asked, citizens in each country were asked whether a list of 20 issues should be best dealt with at the national or EU level. The UK and Denmark wanted three-quarters of the issues dealt with at the national level, with Spain (11), Portugal (10), Greece and Germany (9) desiring a greater national base for decision making than the EU average (8), whilst Belgium (5) and Italy (4) appeared to value their national self-determination less than EU institutions (Eurobarometer 1994, A34). Worryingly, UK citizens' desires to keep defence policy, control over the national currency, the power to tax UK citizens through VAT, industrial policy, immigration and political asylum policy, and the fight against unemployment in national hands are not shared by their EU partners, where those desiring to transfer powers to the EU are in a majority. Clearly, UK voters, together with their Danish, Spanish, Portuguese, Greek and German counterparts, want a looser European co-operation arrangement than do many within the union. An EU opinion poll further confirmed the opposition of Danish, UK and German voters to the establishment of a single currency, with 73%, 61% and 58% of these citizens against this development. Over the EU as a whole, 40% of all citizens are against the proposed single currency (Europinion 1994).

The difficulties experienced in persuading the people of Europe to ratify the Maastricht Treaty caught the European élite by surprise. It became increasingly clear, during this process, that the electorates were not enamoured with what the political élites had cobbled together and with the general integrationist momentum. The surprising narrowness of the French referendum, and the difficulty in persuading Denmark to accept the Maastricht Treaty even at the second time of asking, after substantial opt-outs from the more disagreeable parts of the Treaty, highlighted the reluctance of ordinary voters within many EU countries to follow their business and political élites. This was clear at the supposed heart of Europe when the Northern League in Italy received 6.6% and the Europe of Nations Party, headed by Sir James Goldsmith, received over 12% of the vote in the 1994 French Euro-elections. Similarly Jacques Chirac increased his support in the French presidential elections by espousing a more sceptical opinion on future European integration. The Scandinavian green and left parties presented a popular anti-EU platform, with the Norwegian Centre Party leading the successful opposition to EU membership and followed by anti-EU candidates winning half of the seats in the first Swedish Euro-elections in 1995. Furthermore, discussion of alternatives to current EU policies within both the Conservative and Labour parties in the UK suggests that opposition to further European integration is becoming increasingly popular across Europe.

Lukewarm endorsement of the Maastricht Treaty may signify an increased resistance to further moves towards closer integration amongst large segments of member state citizens, implying a more difficult period for the EU. Within each country there are groups which do well out of further integration and those which do badly. The former category tends to include the business élite, well educated professionals and the farming community, whilst the losers are the ordinary citizens. Perhaps it is not surprising, therefore, that the eloquence with which pro-integration arguments are presented is generally superior to the opposition amongst ordinary voters, yet the actual balance of opinion is nowhere near as one sided.

Organised business in Sweden made crude threats that if EU membership was not supported in that country's referendum, large Swedish companies would invest overseas thereby causing domestic economic stagnation and unemployment. Similar veiled threats have been made by members of the business élite in Germany and elsewhere in attempts to structure European developments in ways which best suit them. Yet, despite this pressure, the result of the Swedish referendum was unconvincing, and subsequent opinion polls suggest that if the referendum was held again the result would be reversed with 62% against membership and only 28% in favour (Guttman 1995). Similarly, the Swiss rejection of the EEA and the Norwegian repeat of its 1972 rejection of EU membership, suggests that support for further integration is perilously split in most European nations, whilst continued unconditional support for the process is something politicians must assume at their peril.

The problems inherent within the chosen policy aims of the EU highlight the practical difficulties in pursuing European integration. The SIM will exacerbate existing regional inequalities within Europe, resulting in a core who benefit from further developments and a periphery who do not. EMU assumes the existence of real economic convergence between countries to secure the long-term sustainability of a single currency. However, it does not presently exist and with weaker nations having to place their economies within the straitjacket of EMU, they are unlikely to be able to rival Germany's economic achievements in the coming years. The Maastricht fiscal convergence criteria paradoxically make productive convergence more difficult since they place weaker economies into a deflationary spiral which hampers, rather than promotes, the faster economic growth needed to catch up with stronger countries.

The enlargement of the EU increases the un-governability of the union. The extension of majority voting might deal with this problem, but it infringes upon national interests whilst exacerbating the conflict between small and large nations over the balance of influence over EU decision-making (Baimbridge & Burkitt 1995b). The EU could expand to include all the former East European countries and if requests for membership were accepted from the former Yugoslavian and Soviet Union states, Turkey, Malta and Cyprus, the EU may conceivably include an association of over 40 individual nations, each with its own different traditions and objectives. Attempts to mould these diverse peoples' into one *de facto* state with a parliament and Council of Ministers intended to represent them all appear unlikely to succeed.

These arguments paint a realistic picture of an integrationist project which is both unpopular amongst a considerable proportion of EU citizens and likely to become more so once its problems intensify with further momentum. However, whilst the EU could implode under the weight of unobtainable aims and unsustainable means, this possibility must not lead to an acceptance of its inevitability; it would be dangerous to write-off the persistence of supporters of European integration who often ignore economic rationality to pursue their ends.

Britain has consistently underestimated the degree of integrationist momentum within the EU. Even though the Treaty of Rome included a commitment to create a political and economic union, UK politicians did not take the aim seriously. At the time of the 1975 referendum, if UK voters had believed they were committing themselves to a political union, and not simply a wider free trade area, few doubt that the vote might have been very different. However, most people accepted the assurances of Edward Heath and others that the EU was not about political integration because it was not thought a practical proposition irrespective of what was written in the Treaty of Rome.

Similarly, the insertion of further integrationist momentum within the Single European Act and the Maastricht Treaty was assumed to be mere rhetoric, impracticable to implement. The ignominious semi-collapse of the ERM in 1992 and 1993 was thought to have ended the prospect of EMU for the rest of this century. However, such views appear to be wishful thinking, as the EU Commission remains confident that economic recovery should enable a majority of member states to achieve the convergence criteria by 1999. Member states suffering most from restrictive economic policies advocated by the EU, including France as its 'franc-fort' policy has driven up unemployment, also appear prepared to accept a continuation of this suffering in order to support European integration. Accordingly, eighteen of the UK's largest banks have established special teams to prepare for the possible arrival of a single currency in 1999, whilst the UK is represented on the EU Monetary Committee which is currently preparing for EMU. Elmar Brok, German Christian Democratic MEP and one of the two European Parliamentary representatives on the preparatory committee of the 1996 Inter-Governmental Conference (IGC), stated that:

"the British government is in grave danger – once again – of

underestimating the degree of common thinking on 1996 and the
future of Europe between France and Germany."

(cited in the *Guardian* 17/2/1995).

Far from the political impetus for further integration subsiding, the European Socialist Group wants closer political union to emerge from the 1996 IGC, with extensions of majority voting in the Council of Ministers and more power for the European Parliament. The British Labour Party MEPs group has accepted and signed this declaration. Moreover, the Christian Democratic parties of Europe, which includes the British Conservative MEPs, recently made clear that they want closer political and economic union despite the Conservative Party's doubts about these issues. Furthermore, despite the departure of Delors, the new EU Commission President, Jacques Santer, has unequivocally stated his clear aim to be:

"*... no departing from the path towards economic and monetary union mapped out in the [Maastricht] Treaty, based on the strict application of the convergence criteria laid down.*"

(cited in the *Guardian* 28/1/1995)

Underestimating such intensity of belief has led us to the verge of EMU and open discussions within the EU about how (not whether) to organise a common foreign policy, establish a European army and bring an increasing amount of decisions currently undertaken by member states under the control of the EU central bureaucracy. Most EU member states' actions demonstrate a fundamental belief that the response to any failure of the integrationist project is to intensify, rather than to reconsider, it.

The immediate hurdles faced by EMU are located in France and Germany. The French government is currently trying to meet the Maastricht criteria in the teeth of intense public opposition. The outcome is as yet unclear, but France possesses a strong executive, who have such an investment in EU-induced misery, that the dice are loaded in favour of restrictive fiscal policy. Whether the German élite can maintain the support of its electorate is more problematic. In an attempt to do so, German bankers and politicians are attempting to tighten the Maastricht criteria; to the extent that they succeed, the less acceptable these criteria become to the rest of the EU.

Replicating the ostrich burying its head in the sand to wait whilst impractical and economically damaging policies collapse may be a comfortable option, but it abdicates the responsibility to put forward alternatives to the current integrationist ideology. Allowing current policies to proceed will damage international relations and set people against each other, by exacerbating inequalities and depressing peripheral European regions, whilst taking from them the economic instruments to make democratic self-determination a practical strategy (Connolly 1995). Despair at the ineffectiveness of democracy to solve problems of mass unemployment and poverty led to the rise of fascism across much of Europe once this century; it must not happen again (Burkitt, Baimbridge & Macey 1994).

The past, present and future policies advocated by the Commission and the dominant Franco-German axis must be analysed, costed and contrasted with alternative approaches which could achieve similar or superior goals more efficiently. The agenda cannot be left to the European political élite to set as it chooses, unless the peoples of Europe, despite being uneasy with the policies pursued in their name, simply assume that there is no alternative. Democracy is based upon informed individuals making a from amongst alternative options. Therefore, the wider economic position of Britain as an outward looking nation must not be overshadowed by the disproportionate focus upon the misconceived process of EU integration.

CHAPTER V

The Detrimental Impact of EU Membership upon the UK's Relationship with the Rest of the World

INTRODUCTION

The extent to which the UK has focused upon its relationship with the EU in the last two decades was out of proportion to the benefits which were assumed to flow from membership and participation in ever-increasing integration. Apart from the fact that the disadvantages clearly outweigh the advantages, such preoccupation with the EU distracted the UK from more beneficial trade and co-operation with other nations. Rather than opponents of further European integration being parochial 'little Englanders', it is those who concentrate almost exclusively upon the Continent to the detriment of long standing relations with other nations who are insular. Indeed, it is an insularity which is to the economic detriment of Britain, because it is the non-EU nations which have achieved higher economic growth over the last two decades and are predicted to do so beyond the turn of the century. International free trade in high value-added manufactured goods will form the basis of the UK's future prosperity. Success in this objective is not well served by insular enclosure within 'fortress Europe'.

THE EU IS A LOW GROWTH AREA

One of the initial attractions of EU membership was the fact that the original six EU states had achieved higher economic growth than the OECD average. For example, between 1958 and 1973,

Table 5.1

Growth and Unemployment in EU and non-EU States

	GDP Growth p.a. (1990–94) volume	Unemployment (% of working population)			
		1991	1992	1993	1994
OECD	1.70	7.4	7.8	7.8	7.8
Major 7	1.73	6.9	7.0	6.9	6.8
EU	1.10	9.4	9.7	11.4	11.3

Source: OECD Main Economic Indicators 1995
[NOTE: EU enlargement to 15 affects figures in 1993–4].

the original six members enjoyed a combined average growth rate of 5.1% per annum (Nevin 1990, 352–3). However, by the time the UK joined, the underlying conditions creating this preferable development had become exhausted, and the EU's restrictive policies produced lower growth and higher unemployment. Thus, the EU became a low growth area and the UK, despite the benefits of North Sea Oil, has been a low growth economy within the EU. As a consequence of two decades of relatively low growth, the EU suffers from very high levels of unemployment (Table 5.1).

THE INTERNATIONALLY FASTEST GROWTH AREAS

If the UK decided to lock itself within a trading bloc, it could choose one more successful than the EU. Established UK trading relations with the USA will continue to generate greater benefit than trade concentrated on EU countries, as the USA continues to expand faster than most of the latter. However, the world's most rapidly growing areas are found amongst the developing countries.

During the last decade, the EU's share of world trade has fallen by one quarter; the high value-added technology sector is over one-third larger in the USA and Japan than in Europe. The greatest visible sign of economic weakness is the persistence of mass unemployment within EU nations which is not matched by the North American, Asian 'Tiger' and Latin American areas. Indeed, it is interesting to note that many Commonwealth countries offer potentially faster growing markets than do other EU member states.

Historic links with Commonwealth nations could give the UK a potential advantage in establishing trading links with these dynamic economies. These include Singapore, India, Pakistan, Malaysia, New Zealand, Australia, Canada and the 'new' South Africa. The East Asian link is potentially also important as a bridgehead to closer trading links with China. A recent survey by Price Waterhouse suggested that out of the UK's top 250 quoted companies, 31% have already invested in China and a further 37% intend to do so within two years (cited in the *Sunday Telegraph* 13/11/94). In 1993, Commonwealth countries accounted for 12.8% of all UK exports and 13.1% of UK imports. Between 1991 and 1993 exports to the Tiger economies, North America, Latin America and Eastern Europe rose by 53%, providing two-thirds of the total export gain in this period.

Over the 10 years from 1983 to 1992 £24.8 billion was invested in Commonwealth nations by UK companies, only £5.8 billion less than in the EU and half as much as in the USA, but nevertheless a significant volume for a trading bloc which receives little strategic attention compared with the supposed advantages emanating from the EU. This trade potential is likely to have become even more favourable in 1995 as those regions with close Commonwealth connections out perform the IMF's estimated world growth rate of 3.7%, whilst the USA, Eastern Europe and non-EU industrial countries were all anticipated to grow faster than the EU.

Moreover, the World Bank (1993) estimated that the areas of the world which grew most during the past two decades, namely South and East Asia, will continue to expand more rapidly in the

Table 5.2

Real GDP Growth, annual average (%)

Countries	Actual 1974–1993	Forecast 1994-2003
Rich Industrial Countries	2.9	2.7
Developing Countries	3.0	4.8
East Asia	7.5	7.6
South Asia	4.8	5.3
Latin America	2.6	3.4
East Europe & former USSR	1.0	2.7
Sub-Saharan Africa	2.0	3.9
Middle East & North Africa	1.2	3.8

Source: World Bank & *The Economist* 1/10/1994

next decade (Table 5.2). Additionally, growth potential is expected to result in significantly higher rates amongst most developing, than amongst the developed, economies. Latin America, Africa and the Middle East join Asia in offering UK companies superior potential for increased export sales than does the EU single market. OECD nations are expected to grow more slowly than developing countries, with EU members more sluggish than the rest of the OECD, so that the focus for UK companies wishing to expand sales overseas must be where demand is rising the fastest. Because of developments in the world economy, the danger of the single market is that it might distract UK firms from pursuing their widest options for sales and encourage a parochial European mentality at a time when a more international focus is indicated, for both short- and long-term trade prospects.

Since Asia and Latin America are the world's fastest growing economies, their purchase of world exports is also likely to increase. In 1993, one-fifth of UK exports, amounting to 4% of GDP, went to developing countries. Because of the rapid growth of these economies, their share of exports will rise and become more important for UK economic development than the EU single market within a relatively short period of time. However, the UK is distracted from taking advantage of such export opportunities by the publicity given to the SIM and by the EU's common external tariff. The latter is an impediment to free trade which encourages other nations to place tariffs upon EU nations' exports, thereby putting UK exporters at a competitive disadvantage with the rest of the world.

PROBLEMS OF ENLARGEMENT
THAT THE EU HAS FAILED TO COUNTER

After the accession of Austria, Finland and Sweden, further EU enlargement will be concentrated, largely though not entirely, in Central and Eastern Europe. EU membership is a symbol for these nations of successful reform and re-acceptance within liberal-democratic capitalism. It is primarily to pursue this sense of new identity, with the political stability and economic benefit they hope it will bring, that they have so passionately sought EU membership. However, whilst Germany and the UK have made favourable noises about enlargement, the EU remains cautiously reluctant to propose a timetable or the conditions to be met for their entry.

One obvious reason is the perceived cost to existing EU members if these poorer, more agriculturally-based nations join a predominantly industrial union. Because of their relative poverty, the East European countries would be entitled to the bulk of EU transfers under the Structural and Cohesion funds, leaving Greece, Ireland, Spain and Portugal potentially large losers. However, the environmental costs for East European nations of meeting tighter EU standards will be high. Any derogation's given to prevent these cost burdens from lowering East European economic expansion would undermine the whole intent of the policy whilst giving Eastern companies a cost advantage.

Some estimates put the cost of enlargement at a doubling of the financial contributions from existing members. Alternatively, Anderson & Tyers (1993) suggest that it would cost a massive £30.5 billion per year to support agricultural producer prices and dispose of the surplus produce; an increase of one-third in projected spending on such schemes by the turn of the century. Anderson & Tyers argue this would lead to a net welfare loss of over £6.5 billion per year; for every £1 East European farmers received in benefit from the extension of the CAP, the cost to each EU taxpayer would be £0.91 combined with a cost to each EU consumer of £0.30, a total of £1.21. Thus it would be cheaper to give the money in the form of direct aid.

Four independent reports, commissioned by the EU, estimated that the costs of EU enlargement for the CAP would lie between £10.5 billion to £25.3 billion, effectively doubling its cost to existing member states (Barclay 1995, 7–8). All four reports therefore concluded that fundamental reform of the CAP was a prerequisite to successful entry of East European nations into the EU. They dismissed the development of a separate, cheaper CAP system for the new entrants or a reduced membership without agricultural support being offered to them, as unnecessarily complicated to enforce whilst undermining the harmonisation necessary for the single market's operation. Instead, CAP reform should concentrate on moving support prices closer to world market levels, decoupling compensatory payments from pro-duction and moving responsibility for income support payments and environmental subsidies to national governments.

These unanimous conclusions were categorically rejected by the EU Commission, whose officials were variously quoted as stating "we know more about it than them" and that the reports would "be going straight into the bin". Such outspoken rejection of its own commissioned studies was coupled to the over-optimistic assertion that the reforms forced upon the CAP by the GATT agreement will release £3.3–4.6 billion to fund enlargement. Clearly the interests of the majority of EU member states, who benefit from CAP transfers, override independent economic research and will most certainly submerge UK expressions of concern over the disastrous consequences of enlargement without corresponding reform to accommodate all nations.

Despite an unwillingness to reform the CAP, the EU has responded to the East European countries cost advantages in agricultural production by negotiating association agreements with them which prevent free trade. Far from encouraging them to specialise in areas of economic activity where they possess an advantage, the agreements established quotas and tariffs on agricultural trade which, certainly for Bulgaria and Rumania, were deliberately set below existing trade levels. This does not represent a level playing field or the neighbourly encouragement and co-operation that European integration is supposed to achieve. Moreover, it is economically illiterate, since allowing East European states to expand their agricultural sector would permit them to earn valuable foreign currency to spend on EU capital and consumer products. Such specialisation will lose farming jobs in most EU member states, which are already uncompetitive without CAP subsidies, but provide consumers with cheaper food; it also benefits non-agricultural West European exports, where employment will grow. This is particularly true of the UK which receives less per capita from the CAP than other member states and is well placed to take advantage of export opportunities in the former Communist countries.

East European nations are more likely to specialise in agricultural exports in the short term because their low wages make the production of relatively simple, standardised agricultural commodities at a cost advantage easier. Complex manufactured goods, which require a large initial investment to meet the quality standards of competitors such as Germany, are more difficult to initiate. However, the impact of EU membership upon the already existing industrial capacity in Eastern Europe requires analysis. The inefficient manufacturing base of the former Communist countries will generate an increasing trade deficit with the EU. Such a deficit generates pressure on external currency values, which raises import prices and thus the cost of living. Higher living costs stimulate claims for higher incomes, producing a rise in labour costs and a further decline in competitiveness. Another currency depreciation results, the spiral recommences and a cumulative weakening of the economy occurs. No government can passively accept such a situation and they will attempt to overcome the deficit by stimulating exports. Cost reductions of the required magnitude involve either severe deflation or substantial devaluation; both methods of continuously reducing costs of production create a fall in the already low East European standard of living. Unless acceptance of such a fall in real incomes is forthcoming, the dynamic effects of EU membership for Eastern Europe will be increasingly adverse. A deteriorating balance of trade leads to restrictive government policies which create a fall in production and employment. This process results in a further worsening of the trade deficit which necessitates additional restrictive policies causing low growth and economic decline. The outlook for Eastern Europe, if integrated within the EU, is therefore depressing.

EU enlargement offers little practical help, and threatens many trading dangers, for East European countries. However, their access to the CAP would add to the budgetary burden borne by existing member states. Consequently, the EU must address the issue of expansion to prevent it from becoming a brake on the long-term economic development of both applicant and current member nations. The EU could follow one of three coherent strategies concerning future expansion:

- it can refuse to admit new members by placing impossible burdens of convergence upon would-be entrants to disguise an unwillingness to admit them, despite the dangers of disillusionment such a strategy will bring;

- the EU could admit all the countries who want to join by becoming a free trade area and relinquishing any federalist designs;

- it could revise its existing mechanisms and institutions to become compatible with a greatly enlarged community.

However, given the EU's apparent determination to press on with further integration whatever the cost, and Germany's determination to admit the East European nations speedily, it is likely that enlargement will proceed without such appropriate reforms being made. Given the difficulties of ratifying the Maastricht Treaty, the problems of changing the essential provisions seem insuperable without the existence of an EU-wide decision, which appears impossible in the foreseeable future. Therefore, the most likely occurrence is enlargement within the existing framework, which will prove the most ruinous outcome for EU member states and potential applicants.

SUMMARY

Because of its misguided foreign policy, the UK has attached itself to a slow-growing group of countries, with endemic high unemployment and few opportunities for competitive advantage. The prospective expansion of the EU to encompass the former communist nations of Eastern Europe is economically potentially destructive within the current framework of EU objectives. Despite the government's continual assertion that 'the benefits of EU membership are self-evident' (e.g. Lord Hanley, 3 July 1995, House of Lords), no UK administration has dared to undertake a cost-benefit analysis of the UK's participation in the EU. Clearly the time has come for the UK to restructure fundamentally its relationship with the EU. Alternative political and economic strategies are crucial to preserving UK self-governance and prosperity.

CHAPTER VI

Alternatives
to Further EU Integration

INTRODUCTION

The evidence presented in this study demonstrates that EU membership, and the momentum towards further political and economic integration, has consistently undermined UK national interests. The EU was designed by the founding members to accommodate their perceived shared objectives, which are quite different from those of the UK, in terms of the dominance of CAP expenditure, the UK's inequitably large net budget contributions, the persistent sizeable trade deficit with the EU and the creation of an immigration policy based on land-locked continental countries rather than an island nation. Further measures of integration, including the abolition of exchange controls, the design of the single market, and giving away economic sovereignty through entering the ERM and EMU, may be rational consequences for those EU nations which are locked closely through trade and a shared culture, but are irrational for the UK which conducts the majority of its trade outside the EU (see Chapter III), a proportion which is likely to grow, and possesses closer cultural ties with the USA and Commonwealth countries.

The costs of EU membership exceed any benefits which have accrued to the UK. Should the UK participate in EMU the economic burden will intensify. The devastating claim, made by former Chancellor Norman Lamont, was that:

> "The advantages of the European Union are remarkably elusive... I cannot pinpoint a single concrete economic advantage that unambiguously comes to this country because of our membership."

However, whilst most analysts accept this as an accurate survey, the question that demands an answer is 'What is the alternative?'. Given that the political and economic élite's in most EU countries have consistently supported further integration, for often varied and contradictory reasons, alternatives have rarely been discussed. In the countries which allowed referendums over the Maastricht Treaty, and in the new EU entrants, almost without exception all major political parties, top business people and trade union leaders joined together in an alliance to persuade their reluctant voters to back the integrationist project. Indeed, it is an indication of the deep mistrust of EMU that so many people, against the 'expert' advice and threats of impending economic collapse if integration is not supported, opposed what was forced on them.

Despite the attempts of certain MPs in the UK, who placed conviction ahead of political careers, the debate is still trivialised and the real choices that the UK faces are obscured. Public opinion appears to be opposed to EU political and economic integration, but it seems to be scared of the consequences of the UK withdrawing its membership. To confront such irrational fears of the unknown, four alternative strategies for UK relationships with the EU and the rest of the world are formulated here.

Option One – The Status Quo Strategy

This is the 'stand firm' or 'do nothing' strategy, which possesses precedents wider than the Danish and UK EMU opt-outs. The Edinburgh Agreement, for example, was delayed for several months by Italy over a dispute concerning their milk quota and was described as "hostage taking in EU decision-making" by the *Financial Times* (29/3/94). Furthermore, the French earlier refused to permit the creation of additional European Parliament seats until the new European Parliament building was located in Strasbourg. Thus, UK action to prevent further integration through the use of its veto, or opting out of any additional supporting measures, could not bring criticism from other EU member states without the application of double standards on their part. However, the strategy rests upon the premise that

86

maintaining EU membership at its current status is both desirable and tenable, which is refuted by the available evidence. The cost of the CAP to taxpayers and consumers, and the problems of trading within the EU from a position of economic weakness, undermine the attraction of the status quo.

The Treaty of Rome prevents a national economic strategy being implemented because it demands the free movement of goods, services, capital and labour, which infringes upon national interests where these are better served by placing restrictions upon such movements. Whilst the movement of goods and services is often preferable to restrictions, the principle is not absolute. Keynes[†] demonstrated, for instance, that protectionist policies could achieve full employment. Similarly, although the unimpeded movement of capital is conventionally assumed to be desirable, it can be destabilising for an economy which is damaged by a flow of 'hot' capital searching for a temporary profitable haven.

Moreover, the *status quo* strategy (excluding further integration) generates limited advantages. It avoids any additional costs of EMU and suggestions of moving towards a common defence and foreign policy position determined by the Commission. It also avoids the extension of QMV which would accelerate the erosion of member states' ability to exercise their sovereignty. It is perhaps the easiest position for politicians to defend, since it means doing nothing new and therefore avoids offending any section of their own parties. However, the strategy is fraught with dangers. While further integration measures can be vetoed, and the UK can avoid participating in future experiments which damage its economic potential, it remains committed to the ones which already exist. The UK's opt-outs do not look secure; for instance, the Commission can circumvent the UK's opt-out from the social chapter by tabling the legislation under the health and safety dimension which is decided by majority voting. The UK is thus powerless to avoid accepting such measures.

[†] In the first Finlay lecture, 'National Self-Sufficiency', at University College, Dublin, 17th April 1933.

The opt-out of EMU is problematic on two grounds. First, ratification of the Maastricht Treaty still commits the UK to adhere to the conditions for economic convergence it establishes, even though Britain may decide not to participate in a single currency. Accordingly the UK will still be reported to the Commission, if it does not keep its budget deficit below 3% of GDP, its public debt below 60% of GDP, its interest rates close to the EU average and if it does not rejoin the ERM. The opt-out simply negates the Maastricht Treaty's insistence that countries must join EMU if they meet these conditions, but the UK cannot adopt a general opt-out from the whole process. If the UK refuses to be pushed into a single currency, its economic policy will remain constrained by the Maastricht Treaty and it will be prevented from pursuing an independent strategy. ERM membership ensures that sterling is fixed at a set rate to the ECU single currency; without the permission of other EU member states, it cannot be devalued, so that the UK would suffer from a *de facto* single currency whether or not it wanted one. Such an outcome is plainly undemocratic. If a collective decision was taken to retain an independent economic stance, it would be farcical to discover that no effective choice existed anyway.

The second problematic aspect of the UK's opt-out of EMU is the degree to which other EU member states have a clear interest that it be negated or even withdrawn and it has been mooted that the opt-out could be declared invalid. Clearly, such pressure upon the UK to join other EU nations would intensify closer to the date for EMU. Denmark possesses a similar opt-out and new EU members such as Austria and Sweden are lukewarm about joining a single currency. The latter actively sought Danish-style opt-outs during its membership negotiations, but all three new EU members were given no choice but to participate in EMU when their economies meet the convergence criteria. Thus, whilst the UK could theoretically refuse to join EMU, many countries are compelled to participate and for this reason alone would not want anyone to benefit at their expense from remaining outside. On a more practical level, the UK has given large sums of money to those EU institutions examining how a single currency could be implemented and Bank of England representatives discuss the UK's accommodation within the European Central Bank. Whilst such manoeuvres are defended as 'keeping UK options open', it is bizarre for a country with no national self-interest in EMU to go through the motions of preparing for it unless some influential figures want to enter EMU despite its enormous cost!

With the UK's opt-out under pressure from sections of the EU-orientated political élite, and with the costs of EU membership far exceeding any expected long term benefits, the *status quo* strategy is fraught with political tensions and persistent disadvantages. Under such circumstances, and with further EU integration implying a deteriorating UK economic environment, alternative strategies should be actively considered.

Option Two – Reduce Membership to the European Economic Area (EEA): "The Norwegian Option"

This strategy avoids conflict with other EU nations over the legitimacy of the opt-outs and cannot be undermined by UK governments being forced to accept rules and regulations imposed by the Commission on a majority vote. As a member of the EEA, the UK would possess full access to the SIM and retain some influence over the rules which affect trade with EU nations. The EEA ensures free trade without the discrimination against external nations created by a customs union. The terms of the EEA stipulate that the UK business sector would operate under the same general conditions as its EU competitors, whilst ensuring that EEA member states develop relevant legislation jointly without the EU imposing standards arbitrarily. The EEA provides member states with the right to oppose and veto EU law if they feel that it operates against their national interest. It also offers the possibility to participate in EU research projects and co-operation on the environment and the social dimension of EU legislation should any EEA participant find these beneficial. A net transfer of income to the EU budget is part of the requirement for EEA membership, but it would be significantly lower than the high budgetary burden imposed by full EU membership upon

UK taxpayers. Thus, the EEA provides many of the advantages of EU membership without some of the costs.

Option Two is similar to the position of Norway after rejecting EU membership in its November 1994 referendum. Like Norway the UK is a member of NATO, so that it possesses no defence interests served by the EU. Both Norway and the UK enjoy large natural resources which are more efficiently conserved and utilised outside the EU; primarily fishing, oil and natural gas. However, the EEA's perceived disadvantage from Norway's viewpoint is that, since Sweden, Finland and Austria joined the EU, there is a power imbalance between EU states and EFTA/EEA members, which Norway fears will eventually lead to an undermining of many benefits that the agreement currently provides. If the UK reduced its membership to that of EEA status, this problem would be reduced, since the UK and Norway would jointly provide a credible counter-balance to the EU in future negotiations.

Membership of the EEA also releases the UK from pressure to participate in the ERM, stipulated by the Maastricht Treaty, and in eventual EMU. Given the UK's previous unfortunate experience of ERM membership, and the still larger disadvantages it would suffer through EMU, this constitutes a significant advantage. Norway's experience is once again informative (see Table 6.1). In the second half of the 1980s, whilst its economy enjoyed rapid economic growth, Norway decided to peg its currency to the ECU as a precursor to eventual EU membership. However, the strategy soon led to a sharp rise in interest rates, and a collapse in domestic demand so severe that the banking sector fell into crisis; most banks were purchased by the state to prevent a complete financial sector collapse. Consequently a previously rapidly growing economy ground to a halt and unemployment started to rise.

Unencumbered by EU membership, Norway was able to rectify its errors by unpegging its currency and allowing a devaluation to cushion the economy, whilst an independent macroeconomic policy restored internal and external balance. The new approach resulted in a 3.4% growth rate in 1992 which rose to 5.1% in 1994,

Table 6.1

Main economic variables for Norway, 1981-1994

Year	Real GDP Growth (%)	Consumer Inflation (%)	Unemployment (%)
1981	0.9	13.6	1.5
1982	0.3	11.3	2.6
1983	4.5	8.4	3.3
1984	5.6	6.2	3.0
1985	5.4	5.7	2.5
1986	4.2	7.2	2.0
1987	2.0	8.7	2.1
1988	-0.5	6.7	3.2
1989	0.6	4.6	4.9
1990	1.7	4.2	5.2
1991	1.6	3.4	5.5
1992	3.4	2.3	5.9
1993	2.4	2.3	6.0
1994	5.1	1.4	5.4

Sources: OECD Main Economic Indicators, 1981–1995;
EIU Country Reports – Norway, 1986–1995

unemployment at 5.4% and falling, inflation at only 1.4%, a budget deficit expected to be no higher than 2.8% of GDP and a balance of payments surplus of 2.5% of GDP at the end of 1994. The devaluation allowed relative Norwegian unit costs to fall by 8.6% during 1993 and is expected to narrow to 2% above its main competitors by the end of 1995, which is a rapid improvement from an 11% disadvantage in 1977. Thus, freed from restrictive ERM rules which prevent such a coherent economic strategy, Norway was able to avoid the economic costs suffered by the UK due to its ERM membership. The assertion of Norway's political élite, that rejection of EU membership would bring economic disaster was confounded by these events, which demonstrated the superiority of an alternative non-EU economic strategy.

Option Three – Free Trade on Industrial and Financial Commodities: "The Swiss Option"

Since the UK is ill-served by participating in the CAP and the CFP, a restriction of free trade with EU nations to industrial and financial goods and services would prove more beneficial than the present status quo. The remaining EFTA countries negotiated such a free trade agreement with the EU in 1972, after the UK, Denmark and Ireland had joined the EU, thus escaping from the financial burdens and policy constraints imposed by EU membership. As with membership of the EEA, this approach would allow the UK to reorientate its economic policy to serve its own needs rather than those of competitor EU countries. The money saved by non-contribution to the EU budget could be used to increase incentives for productive investment within the UK, and for state expenditure on infrastructural and research-based projects which increase long term competitiveness. This option provides greater freedom than EEA membership, which implies the agreement of common rules and equal conditions for competition, so that greater pressure would be placed upon EEA participants to accept EU regulations to ensure continued co-operation. Restricting EU relations to a free trade agreement would remove the possibility of such behind-the-scenes pressure.

This third option closely resembles Switzerland's current position, after a majority of its citizens and cantons voted against EEA membership in December 1992. This decision was motivated partly by a desire to preserve its 700 year independence from the rest of Europe, and partly by a disillusionment with an EU model which would undermine the country's tradition of direct democracy for a federation operated by an élite largely unaffected by its member states' citizens (*The Economist* 28/11/1992). Although Switzerland's political and business élite favoured EEA membership, the Swiss voters did not agree. Indeed, in March 1995, a referendum voted to ban transit lorry traffic through the Alps by 2004 to force traffic onto the railways. Such democratically inspired national action to safeguard the environment was not welcomed by the EU.

These decisions did not haemorrhage economic vitality; instead they strengthened the Swiss economy. For instance, a sharp influx of foreign funds occurred after the 'No' vote, raising the stock market by 30% and strengthening the value of the Swiss Franc. This allowed Switzerland to maintain the lowest interest rates in Europe, which facilitated investment growth of 2% in 1994 and an estimated 3.5% in 1995. Additionally inflation is expected to remain below 2%, unemployment is only 3.9%, in 1995/6 GDP growth is forecast at 2% and exports to rise by 4% generating a record balance of payments surplus. Thus Switzerland, despite a continued eagerness amongst its political élite for future EU membership, is benefiting from its arm's-length relations.

These relations are based upon over 100 bilateral treaties, including a 1972 Free Trade Agreement which covers industrial goods (Church 1993). Amongst OECD countries, agriculture apart, there is no economy more open to the outside world than Switzerland. Exposure to such competitive pressures encouraged the development of some of the world's most internationally-orientated companies. Switzerland is the fourteenth largest overall trading nation in the world and the second trade partner with the EU (after the USA) and the third largest exporter after the USA and Japan. Consequently non-membership of the EU has failed to hamper its economic development or its trading potential.

Despite economic success outside the EU, the Swiss authorities express two fears, which are familiar to UK citizens when confronted with the possibility of a change in relations with the EU. First, since the majority of trade is done with EU nations, membership is essential to protect it. Second, absence from the EEA will result in EU discrimination against Swiss-made goods through technical barriers. These fears are, however, easily allayed. In the Swiss case only 58% of exports and 71.5% of imports relate to the EU, so that its economy is less orientated towards the EU than most commentators claim. Additionally, like the UK, an increasing proportion of its international trade is being conducted with the fast growth areas in Asia and the USA rather than with the slow-growing EU. Thus Switzerland's dependence upon the EU market is likely to diminish in the future. The trend would be accelerated if the UK, Switzerland's fifth most important trading partner, left the EU.

In answer to the second point, the EU nations benefit far more than Switzerland from their trade so that they are unlikely to engage in discriminatory practices that could endanger their own more sizeable exports. Moreover, the Uruguay GATT agreement prevents arbitrary treatment of a nation's exports in any market, thus preventing active discrimination against Swiss, or any other countries', exports by the EU. Of course unofficial barriers to trade do exist, but EU membership is no guarantee that these will be dismantled. For example, fellow EU nations exporting beer into Germany face stricter purity regulations than the EU has agreed. The direct action of French farmers in destroying UK meat imports whenever they feel their livelihoods are being infringed is a further example of barriers to free EU trade which the French police appear unable to control. EU membership has not proved helpful in avoiding such behaviour.

Option Four – Withdrawal: "The Greenland Option"

The previous options each retain varying constraints imposed by the EU upon the UK's economic behaviour. For instance, the status quo option implies similar costs to EMU unless the UK breaks the Maastricht rules whilst the EEA involves a budgetary cost and a general acceptance of the EU's regulations for the long-term survival of the agreement, which implies a *de facto* submission to the EU on many matters. The Swiss option is the most palatable but if this is achieved with the UK remaining bound by the Treaty of Rome, economic policy remains fundamentally constrained and speculators could therefore 'punish' sterling for non-compliance with EMU rules. Therefore, in view of the varying but substantial costs implied by any form of EU membership, a fourth option for the UK is complete withdrawal, so that it can take back the ability to determine its economic fate. This strategy is supported by the Federation of Small Businesses whilst the Institute of Directors, although opposed to EMU, favours retention of EU membership.

Withdrawal would take the form of Parliament repealing the European Communities Act of 1972 under which EU directives take precedence over UK law, as well as the 1986 and 1993 European Communities (Amendments) Acts which added the Single Market and the Maastricht Treaty. Following the example of Greenland which left the EU after 12 years of membership in 1985, the UK could negotiate a Treaty of Separation to annul the Treaty of Accession and establish formal future trade co-operation on a mutually beneficial basis under the auspices of GATT rules.

Once attained, the UK is free to operate any economic policy it wishes. It could take the form of a determined effort to rebuild large sections of the UK's industrial base, decimated by overall EU membership and latterly accelerated by the ERM. Burkitt, Baimbridge & Reed (1992) outlined the essential elements of one such strategy. However, the crucial point is that UK citizens would possess the power to decide how they are governed and how the economy is run, rather than exercising merely a token vote at election time because important decisions concerning fiscal, monetary, exchange rate and trade policy are taken in Brussels. The economy would be free to react to external shocks in a way which suited its particular circumstances, not what suited Germany as the strongest EU state. Indeed, as the German and Japanese economic 'miracles' were partially based upon a competitive currency and long-term low interest rate industrial finance, the UK could adopt a similar approach to compete more successfully with EU members rather than be restricted by EU economic policies which do not favour it.

The potential of economic independence is unsurprisingly dismissed by supporters of EU integration as illusory. They argue that sterling would be prey to speculation outside the ERM or EMU, requiring higher interest rates to be maintained than would be necessary inside; productive investment is thus deterred. Moreover, they believe that the only way in which the UK can exercise any power in world affairs is as part of the EU, because it is too small to do so on its own. Furthermore, withdrawal may endanger foreign investment in the UK and cause negative reactions from remaining EU members. So successful have these scare tactics been, that even though a majority of people in the UK oppose further integration and many would like to leave the EU when given the chance to achieve this in the 1975 referendum, voters were frightened to exercise their expressed preferences and grudgingly accepted what the political and business élite told them.

Far from the Euro-sceptics having won the battle of ideas, the reverse is actually true. Whilst opinion polls consistently show that UK voters do not like the EU and would be free of it if they had a choice, the supporters of European integration control the agenda so firmly that whenever an opportunity arises to debate Britain's future, citizens are inundated with a welter of the influential telling them that to withdraw would be an economic disaster. Under such circumstances, the real issues are obscured by a focus upon vague statements about 'being at the heart of Europe', or 'better in and influencing things than out in the cold', so that people possess little effective choice.

These scare tactics are, of course, simply that. They enjoy little factual basis and their predictions are unlikely to occur if the UK did withdraw from the EU. For instance, after the ERM debacle, it is disingenuous of the supporters of European integration to suggest that sterling would be damaged by floating. During the two years of being fixed to the other EU currencies, the UK lost over a million jobs, and estimates varying between £4 billion and £15 billion pounds expended in defending sterling's value which could have been devoted to productive ends. It is farcical to suggest that the world's financial markets will be fooled into believing that a permanently fixed exchange rate system will operate better than the ERM, without inflicting permanent damage upon EU countries and regions. International speculation does not occur against currencies set at the equilibrium level nor against rational exchange rate systems, but as with the ERM in the Autumn of 1992, it will undermine any moves towards EMU which are not viable, whatever EU politicians suggest. Destabilising speculation is best prevented by international, not EU, action; perhaps with a tax on currency transactions which are reversed within a short period of time, as mooted by President

Clinton at the time of the ERM crisis. The history of free-floating currencies is not as successful as its advocates often claim, but managed floating is certainly preferable to the damage inflicted by an inflexible single currency.

The argument that the UK can only exercise any influence on world events within the EU is perverse, appearing to be simultaneously defeatist yet hankering for a world leadership role. The UK lost its former world position because of economic problems. Decades of slow economic growth reduced the UK from being the leading world economy before the turn of the century to a medium sized economy in the 1990s, with political power declining in tandem. Japan and Germany obtained increased international influence not because of foreign policy or military might, but because their economic strength compels attention. If the UK is to regain influence, it must be based upon economic success, which is less likely to be secured within the EU straitjacket. Furthermore, the UK could secure international influence far in excess of its size through less conventional means. The Scandinavian countries, for example, achieved significant prestige for their environmental and human rights campaigns. The UK, when it established the NHS, was likewise a model which countless other countries used when constructing their own welfare systems. International influence does not, therefore, have to be of the traditional type. It can be more effectively attained through UK participation in the G7 summits than by being one voice amongst fifteen (or more) within the EU.

The belief that withdrawal would reduce the flow of foreign investment into the UK is widely held, but the analysis of Chapters III and V demonstrates its lack of validity. A UK economy growing faster outside the EU with a permanently competitive exchange rate is more attractive to foreign markets than an EU member state. Nor is the idea that withdrawal from the EU would provoke retaliation from current EU 'partners' any more probable. Apart from EU political pressure attempting to persuade the UK to change its mind, the other EU countries will not engage in a trade war because their surplus with the UK means that it would hurt them most. The UK habitually runs a large trade deficit with the EU, which means that they sell to us more then we sell to them. Consequently it would be self-damaging for the EU to engage in any measures which reduced trade with the UK. Indeed, if the UK could reorientate its economic policy outside the EU to promote greater economic growth, the UK would be able to buy more EU goods than if it stayed a member and remained a low growth economy within a low growth bloc. Thus the UK is in a strong position to bargain with other EU member states. Any impression of the UK as a weak nation, having to accept EU dictates, is a misconception propagated by the enthusiasts for further integration.

Withdrawal from the EU is only a first, necessary step. Once achieved, the UK can develop whatever trading relations with other nations it desires. For instance, one possibility is to rejoin EFTA, so taking advantage of a free trade area without the pretensions of economic and political union. EFTA could be expanded to include those East European nations currently desperate to join the EU as a 'badge' of their market economy credentials, but which the EU is hesitant to admit because of the agricultural costs. An EFTA free trade area in manufactures, without agricultural protection, would assist all nations.

A second alternative could be to reinvigorate the Common-wealth trading bloc (West 1995). Australia, New Zealand and Canada were severely damaged by the UK's decision to join the EU (Burkitt & Baimbridge 1990) and subsequently reorientated much of their trade towards the emerging economies of East Asia. However, ties of language, culture and mutual advantage would ease a resumption of trade between them, other Commonwealth nations and the UK. The Commonwealth is an asset which the UK often underestimates, particularly since it now includes some of the fastest growing economies in the world, which often possess closer links with other fast growth areas than the UK. Con-sequently, reorientation of British trade policy will prove profitable (see Chapter V).

A third alternative is to form an association with the North American Free Trade Agreement (NAFTA), which comprises the USA, Canada and Mexico. Since approximately one quarter of

UK trade is already done with the USA, this bloc, together with the Commonwealth link to Canada, would be beneficial for the UK. Furthermore, talks between the USA, China, Japan and fifteen other Pacific nations concluded with their determination to form a Pacific Free Trade Area by the year 2010 for the industrialised countries, which would encompass most of the fastest growing economies in the world. It is in the UK's economic self-interest to negotiate a trade agreement with such countries rather than to remain within the EU, since the potential for export sales is significantly higher. Consequently, whilst withdrawal from the EU provides the UK with an opportunity to operate an independent trading policy relying upon bilateral agreements with major trading nations, a combination of free trading areas between EFTA, the Commonwealth, NAFTA and in future the Pacific nations would create superior trading opportunities for the UK than remaining trapped within the EU could do.

SUMMARY

The analysis of previous Chapters is clear. Britain has suffered heavy costs as a result of its increasing integration with an internationally slow-growth EU. The weight of evidence suggests that future developments envisaged for the EU, legally enshrined in the Maastricht Treaty, will impose still further burdens upon the UK economy. They also reduce substantially the democratic rights of citizens to economic self-management. The most common response to these facts is to assert that, whatever the burdens, 'there is no alternative' to EU membership. This Chapter demonstrates the weakness of such a claim and outlines various alternative strategies. Remarkably no British government, before or after accession, has conducted an in-depth survey of alternatives to EU integration. Such a neglect for the welfare of UK citizens is inexcusable and its rectification is long overdue.

Conclusion

EU membership implies certain, heavy costs upon Britain. Of the easily measurable costs over the last decade (1985 to 1994), the UK has:

- suffered an overall £89 billion trade deficit with other EU members (£145 billion at today's prices);

- made a net contribution of £30 billion to the EU budget (at current prices);

- lost a minimum of £68 billion as a result of its ERM membership between October 1990 and September 1992 (arising from a 4% rise in unemployment, a 3% increase in interest rates, a fall in output below its trend growth rate and the sterling expended in the doomed bid to defend the exchange rate);

- found its business facing a bill amounting to 8% of its GDP to meet directives emanating from the Commission in Brussels.

Additionally, the National Consumer Council estimated in September 1995 that the CAP adds £20 per week to the food bill for a family of two adults and two children, with the cost rising to £28 per family per week when including the administration costs of the CAP financed through taxation. Moreover, the cost in highly-paid ministerial and civil service time of attempting to devise EU-wide policies is substantial. It has been estimated that 70% of the Ministry of Agriculture's workload is now Brussels-related, whilst at each of the Departments of Environment and Trade and Industry this figure is around 30%, and in the Treasury, 15%.

These statistics demonstrate the damage wrought by EU membership upon the UK economy. However, the future burden imposed by EMU will be higher, consisting of two principle elements; the effect of meeting and maintaining the Maastricht fiscal convergence criteria as a condition for EMU entry and the impact of a single currency once established.

EMU perhaps most fundamentally impacts upon the ability of a nation state to design and operate its own economic policy in the interests of its own citizens. Governments should attempt to utilise all economic instruments available to ensure optimum economic prosperity, full employment and low inflation. This means that fiscal and monetary policy, including the ability to vary interest rates and the exchange rate, should be concentrated upon achieving these internal economic goals and not have their effect weakened by additional requirements to maintain external currency levels or meet arbitrary targets such as prescribed by the Maastricht Treaty.

The argument that a country should operate its economic policy in its own national interests appears an obvious statement, however EMU would, by definition, impose significant constraints upon any participating nation's ability to achieve its goals. Recognition of this fact is not particularly new, and indeed Lord Keynes expressed the argument eloquently, speaking in the House of Lords on 23rd May 1944, when he stated that governments should ensure that:

> "... the external value of sterling shall conform to its internal value as set by our domestic policies, and not the other way round. Secondly, we intend to retain control of our domestic rate of interest, so that it keeps as low as suits our purposes without interference from the ebb and flow of international capital movements of flights of hot money. Thirdly, whilst we intend to prevent inflation at home, we will not accept deflation at the dictate of influences from outside. In other words, we abjure the instruments of bank rate and credit creation operating through the increase of unemployment as a means of forcing our domestic economy into line with external factors."

A Treasury Green Paper (Cmnd. 7405), published in 1978, accepted the case that participation in the then European Monetary System would be against the British national interests.

Its arguments remain valid against EMU, which similarly yet permanently fails to:

- lay a foundation for higher employment and economic growth; rather it sets constraints on both;

- impose obligations on its stronger members symmetrical to those falling on weaker economies;

- provide for realignments of exchange rates when changing underlying economic circumstances make these desirable.

A single currency cannot end recessions. When they occur, they affect countries to different degrees, and EMU will restrict government's ability to respond flexibly. EMU directly constrains monetary, as well as indirectly limiting budgetary, policy options. Consequently, all the burden of adjustment in a recession will fall on output and jobs. This deflationary bias lies at the heart of EMU.

Without a coherent strategy for dealing with Brussels, based upon a recognition of the immense opportunities awaiting an independent Britain, the incremental pressure of events tends to generate a drift towards conformity with EU decisions. The integrationist spiral, fuelled by the French-German alliance and the Commission, possesses a self-reinforcing mechanism of its own. However, by taking the path towards a single currency, the EU inadvertently re-opened a fundamental debate, since EMU irresistibly propels political integration. As Nigel Lawson observed on the 25th January 1989:

"Economic and monetary union is incompatible with sovereign states with control over their own fiscal and monetary policies."

In March 1996, the British Prime Minister will gather with fellow EU heads of government in Turin to open the next European Inter-Governmental Conference (IGC). The surrounding publicity will revive EU issues as UK pre-election campaigning warms up. Consequently, all political parties require both a coherent position and an internal consensus on negotiating objectives with the EU. EMU may ultimately implode through its inherent contradictions, but Britain could hasten this outcome through purposive action.

The December 1995 EU summit in Madrid confirmed that the key political condition for EMU, a functioning Franco-German axis committed to it, remains intact. If EMU does not occur in 1999, it will not be for lack of determination in Paris and Bonn. The implications for Britain are enormous, because the re-affirmation of French and German prioritisation of EMU has left the UK assumption that a single currency is doomed to fail looking problematic. Muddling along in the hope that the single currency decision will go away was never, and can no longer be presented as, a coherent policy. The benefits of EMU have long been a virtually unchallenged article of faith for the French and German political classes; by confirming detailed plans for transition, they seek to silence democratic debate about the wisdom of the 1999 timetable. In Madrid they displayed the blind arrogance of power to public opinion by, in effect, proclaiming: 'it does not matter whether the policy of meeting the Maastricht requirements make sense to our people: we know better and intend to pursue it'.

To avoid such arrogance and to restore self-government to the UK, Section 2(2) of the 1972 European Communities Act, which makes EU decisions binding in Britain, must be repealed. The repeal would be an enabling measure, permitting the UK government to undertake whatever policies are deemed necessary in the national interest, without fear of challenge in UK courts or of an adverse judgement by the European Court. Short of withdrawal, the UK government, as a minimum negotiating position to restore democratic accountability, should:

- repudiate a single currency. EMU transfers economic power from the people to non-elected institutions such as the European Central Bank and the European Commission;

- end the Commission's ability to propose legislation. Unelected civil servants should only administer laws;

- transfer control of agricultural and fishing policy back to the people through their national elected parliaments;

- press for repatriating authority currently wielded by Brussels back to Britain, so that 'subsidiarity' means not just no further centralisation but a diminution of existing EU competence;

- allow national parliaments to over-rule the decisions of the European Court of Justice. Unelected judges should not make or interpret laws and EU directives in such a way as to impose financial and legal obligations upon member states without their consent. Legislation should be the prerogative of democratic governments.

Pursuit of such policies at the 1996 IGC will enable the UK to reduce trade barriers with Eastern Europe, to negotiate a North Atlantic or Commonwealth free trade area and to develop a programme to regenerate British industry. It could avoid the deflationary impact of the Maastricht Treaty, which is currently lengthening dole queues and undermining prosperity. The UK's historic role is not to run with the herd pretending EMU can be effective in its current form; rather it is to assert what a fundamentally divisive project it will be.

The UK occupies a strong bargaining position should it decide to withdraw from the EU. It is a major contributor to the EU budget, the only net EU consumer of many of its surplus agricultural commodities, an overwhelming importer of EU manufacturers, the largest provider of fishing waters and the only EU country self-sufficient in energy. Eighty per cent of UK assets lie outside Europe; half are in the USA and approximately one-third in the Commonwealth and the emerging markets. The invisible earnings flowing from these assets exceed the UK's entire income from manufacturing exports and are almost as large as its total visible trade. Consequently the new reality is that Britain's total earnings from outside the EU are almost 50% higher than those from within it. Concentration upon an EU that represents only a minority of British interests is contra-indicated. Any notion that the UK is a helpless supplicant without alternatives to EU membership is sharply refuted by the facts.

The impact of 'globalisation' upon the nation state is frequently exaggerated; it narrows options, but does not remove them. Nor are national cultures, economies and politics as porous before the march of the international marketplace as orthodoxy insists. For instance, advertisers have found that global campaigns do not carry universal appeal and consumption patterns vary significantly throughout Europe with respect to many staple items, including food, housing and entertainment. Moreover, the latest evidence is that multinationals are de-globalising their production, pulling back into their home regions. Even the financial markets are rooted in national economies, with their divergent pre-occupations. The political community represented by the nation state remains the firmest building block for collective action, despite constraints on its power. No movement nor development threatens the nation's dominance anywhere except in the EU, where federalist contradictions have been increasingly demonstrated in recent years. The global problems which are beyond the capacity of the nation state to resolve, such as currency realignment and environmental protection, do not indicate EU membership, because regional blocs are similarly ineffective. Only truly international action can be decisive in these spheres. Britain can promote such action at least as effectively outside the EU and perhaps more so once freed from concentrating upon EU-generated problems.

Should EMU ever be implemented, it would inevitably lead to political integration. Monetary union acceptable to Germany involves the imposition of rigorous budgetary discipline, which requires centralised direction and co-ordination. Such a potential development highlights the most fundamental issue; whether the British electorate retains the power to determine its domestic economic policy and its standard of living. Such a basic freedom is undermined by the Maastricht Treaty, which hands the final determination over monetary measures to unelected central bankers. To those who value democratic citizenship, such decisions incur consequences far too significant for living standards to be left to central bankers.

Therefore, EMU threatens not only living standards but also the right of people in democracies to govern themselves. The changes it generates will mean that, whenever the House of

Commons fulfils its constitutional role of brining citizens' complaints to the attention of executive authority, no effective response is possible since power has moved to EU institutions. Britain must, therefore, make a clear statement expressing its opposition to any future erosion of the ability of its people to govern themselves and to rebuild its industrial strength. This would uncouple the UK from damaging integrationist trends, whilst allowing it to seize the global opportunities open to it as an internationally competitive but independent country. Such a major change in strategy requires determination and far-sighted thinking by both political leaders and people. The prize, however, is great. It is no less than the survival of Britain as an economically prosperous and democratically self-government nation.

BIBLIOGRAPHY

Anderson, K. & Tyers, R. (1993), 'Implications of EC Expansion for European Agricultural Policies, Trade and Welfare', *Centre for Economic Policy Research,* Discussion Paper 829.

Bakhoven, A.F. (1989), 'The Completion of the Single Market in 1992: Macroeconomic Consequences for the European Community', *Central Planning Bureau,* No. 56, The Netherlands.

Barclay, C. (1995), 'The Common Agricultural Policy and Eastern Europe', *House of Commons Library Research Paper,* No. 13, House of Commons, London.

Bayoumi, T. & Eichengreen, B. (1992), 'Is there a conflict between EC Enlargement and European Monetary Unification?', *CEPR Discussion Paper,* No. 646.

Berry, R., Kitson, M. & Michie, J. (1995), 'Towards Full Employment: the first million jobs', *Full Employment Forum,* London.

Baimbridge, M. & Burkitt, B. (1995a), 'Equitable Voting in the EU?: Options for Change', *Politics,* Vol. 15, No. 2, pp. 79–87.

Baimbridge, M. & Burkitt, B. (1995b), 'Council of Ministers Voting Rights', *Politics Review,* Vol. 4, No. 3, pp. 31–33.

Baimbridge, M. & Burkitt, B. (1995c), 'Central Bank Independence: A New Non-Inflationary Beginning or Democratic Deficit?', *Briefing Notes in Economics,* Vol. 18, No. 5, pp. 1–4.

Booker, C. & Jamieson, B. (1994), 'How Europe Cost us £235bn', *Sunday Telegraph,* 9 October.

Burkitt, B. & Baimbridge, M. (1990), 'The Performance of British Agriculture and the Impact of the Common Agricultural Policy: A Historical Review', *Rural History,* Vol. 1, No. 2, pp. 265–280.

Burkitt, B. & Baimbridge, M. (1991), 'The Cecchini report and the Impact of 1992', *European Research,* Vol. 2, part 5, pp. 16–19.

Burkitt, B. & Baimbridge, M. (1994a), 'Full Employment and Exchange Rate Competitiveness', *Employment International,* January, pp. 43–56.

Burkitt, B. & Baimbridge, M. (1994b), 'An Independent Central Bank: An End to Democratic Economic Policies?', *Full Employment Forum,* Discussion Paper No. 4, Watford, 1994.

Burkitt, B. & Baimbridge, M. (1995a), 'Reflections on Central Bank Independence', *The Review of Policy Issues,* Vol. 1, No. 3, pp. 29–40.

Burkitt, B. & Baimbridge, M. (1995b), 'A Reply to Professor Dowd', *The Review of Policy Issues,* Vol. 1, No. 3, pp. 47–51.

Burkitt, B., Baimbridge, M. & Macey, M. (1995), 'The European Parliamentary Election of 1994 and Racism in Europe', *Ethnic & Racial Studies,* Vol. 18, No. 1, pp. 128–130.

Burkitt, B., Baimbridge, M. & Macey, M. (1994), 'The Maastricht Treaty: Exacerbating Racism in Europe?', *Ethnic & Racial Studies,* Vol. 17, No. 3, pp. 420–441.

Burkitt, B., Baimbridge, M. & Mills, J. (1993), *What Price the Pound? – The Exchange Rate and Full Employment,* Full Employment Forum, Watford.

Burkitt, B., Baimbridge, M. & Reed, S. (1992), *From Rome to Maastricht: A Reappraisal of Britain's Membership of the European Community,* Campaign for an Independent Britain, London.

Cambridge Econometrics (1990), *Regional Economic Prospects,* Cambridge University Press, Cambridge.

Cecchini, P. (1988), The European Challenge – the benefits of a single market, Wildwood House, Aldershot.

Church, C. (1993), 'Switzerland and Europe: Problem or Pattern?', *European Policy Forum.*

Connolly, B. (1995), *The Rotten Heart of Europe – The Dirty War for Europe's Money,* Faber & Faber, London.

Court of Auditors (1995), 'Annual report concerning the financial year 1994 together with the institutions' replies', *Official Journal of the European Communities,* Vol. 38, No. C303, 14 November, pp. 1–328.

CSO 1995, *Family Spending – a report on the 1994–95 Family Expenditure Survey,* HMSO, London.

DeGrauwe, P. (1992), *The Economics of Monetary Integration,* Oxford University Press, Oxford.

Delors, J. (1989), *Report on Economic and Monetary Union in the European Community,* Office for Official Publications, Luxembourg.

EC Commission (1970), 'Economic and Monetary Union in the Community (Werner Report)', *Bulletin of the European Communities,* Supplement No. 7, OOPEC, Brussels.

EC Commission (1988), 'The Economics of 1992', *European Economy,* No 35, Brussels.

EC Commission (1990), 'One Money, One Market', *European Economy,* No. 44, Brussels.

EU Commission (1995), *European Economy – Economic Trends,* No. 4/5, European Commission, Brussels.

Eurobarometer (1993), *Trends 1974–1992,* Eurobarometer, Brussels.

Eurobarometer (1994), *Report No. 41,* April–May, Eurobarometer, Brussels.

Europinion (1994), Opinion Poll, 1–5 December 1994.

Ersboll, N. & Ludlow, P. (1995), *Preparing for 1996 and a larger European Union,* Centre for European Policy Studies, Brussels.

Frankel, J.A. and Wei, S.J. (1993), *Trade Blocs and Currency Blocs,* CEPR Conference on The Monetary Future of Europe, La Coruna, Spain, December.

Guttman, R. J., 1995, 'New EU member seeks influence', *Europe,* September, pp. 9–10.

Holland, S. (1995), 'Squaring the Circle', in Coates, K. & Holland, S. (eds.), *Full Employment for Europe,* Spokesman, Nottingham.

Hopkins, S. (1995), 'The Council of Ministers', *Politics Review,* Vol. 4, No. 3, p. 32.

Johnson, G., 1991, *World Agriculture in Disarray,* Macmillan, London.

Jones, L. (1995), 'Europe not Maastricht', *Socialist Campaign Group News,* July, p. 11.

Lockwood, C. (1994), 'Play the EU Game; You can Waste Millions', *Daily Telegraph,* 16 November.

MacDougall, D. (1977), *The Role of Public Finance in the European Communities,* Office for the Official Publications of the European Communities, Brussels.

MacDougall, D. (1992), 'Economic and Monetary Union and the European Community Budget', *National Institute for Economic Review,* May, pp. 64–68.

Miller, V. & Dyson, J. (1994), 'The European Communities (Finance Bill)', *House of Commons Library Research Paper,* No. 94/117, London.

National Consumer Council (1995), *Agricultural Policy in the European Union,* National Consumer Council, London.

Nevin, E. (1990), *The Economics of Europe,* Macmillan, London.

Sapir, A., Sekkhat, K. and Weber, A. (1994), *The Impact of Exchange Rate Fluctuations on European Union Trade,* CEPR Discussion Paper, No. 1041.

Sleath, P. (1995), 'Fish Facts' , *European Journal,* March, p. 20.

Taylor, M. (1995), *A Single Currency - Implications for the UK Economy,* Institute of Directors, London.

Tobin, J. (1994), 'Speculators' Tax', *New Economy,* Vol. 1, pp. 104–109.

West, K. (1995), *Economic Opportunities for Britain and the Commonwealth,* Royal Institute for International Affairs, London.

World Bank (1993), *The East Asian Miracle – Economic Growth and Public Policy,* Oxford University Press, Oxford.